Nature's OFFERINGS

PRIMITIVE PROJECTS INSPIRED BY THE FOUR SEASONS

BY MAGGIE BONANOMI

Nature's
OFFERINGS

Nature's OFFERINGS

PRIMITIVE PROJECTS INSPIRED BY THE FOUR SEASONS
BY MAGGIE BONANOMI

Editor: Deb Rowden

Designer: Brian Grubb

Photography:
Aaron T. Leimkuehler

Illustration:
Maggie Bonanomi and
Lon Eric Craven

Technical Editor:
Donna di Natale

Production assistance:
Jo Ann Groves

Published by:
Kansas City Star Books
1729 Grand Blvd.
Kansas City, Missouri, USA 64108

All rights reserved Copyright © 2009
The Kansas City Star Co.

First edition, first printing

ISBN: 978-1-935362-22-7

Library of Congress Control
Number: 2009907128

Printed in the United States of
America by Walsworth Publishing Co.,
Marceline, MO

To order copies, call
StarInfo at
(816) 234-4636 and
say "Books."

PickleDish.com
The Quilter's Home Page

www.PickleDish.com

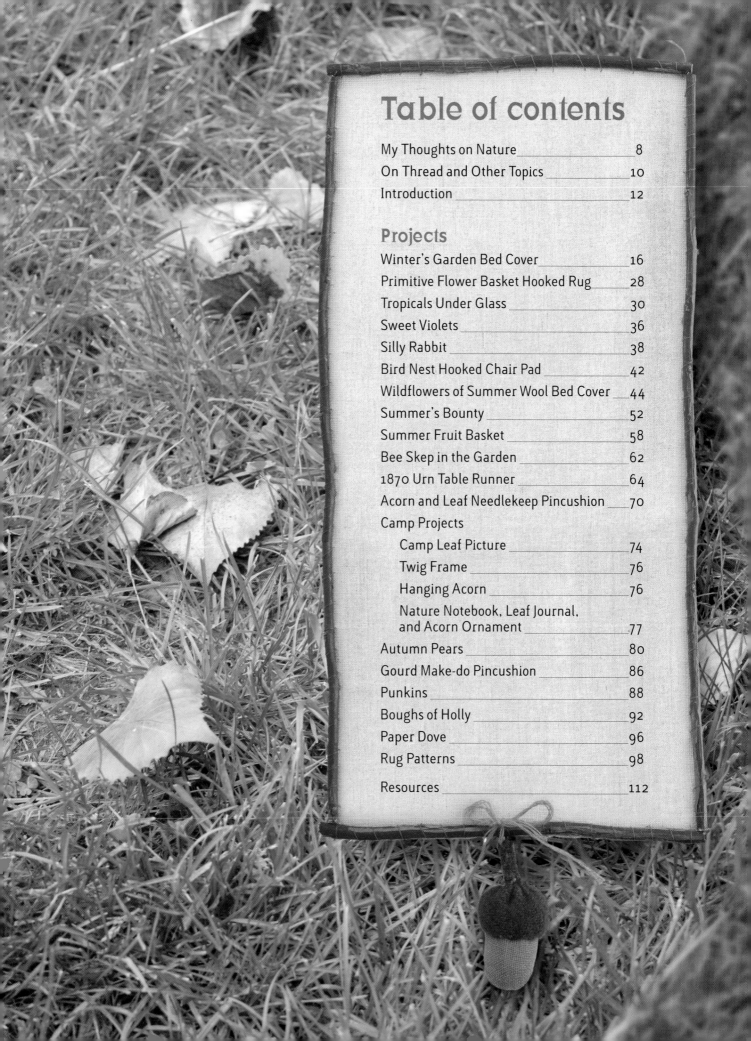

Table of contents

Acknowledgements

Here I am again with so many to thank. First, thanks to Doug Weaver of Kansas City Star Books for giving me the opportunity to do another book.

Thanks to:

Janae Fuller at the Battle of Lexington State Historic Site - for allowing us to use your garden for part of our photo shoot.

My friend Bev Sanders for suggesting using twigs to frame a project in my Camp Projects, it worked perfectly.

Emma Lou Lais - for continuing to share your love of rug hooking and Rhonda Manley and your wonderful studio, Black Sheep Wool Designs. It's the place to go to get inspired by beautiful wool, and I cannot forget the gals at rug hooking for continuing to keep me on task....

Cindi and Tonja at Blackberry Primitives for your wools (I used in the Wildflowers of Summer Wool Bed Cover).

To Darlene Christopherson at Hobbs Bonded Fibers in Waco, TX for sending the cotton batting for my Winter Garden bedcover, it was a pleasure to work with.

Jeanne Horton of Country Sampler in Spring Green, WI - your friendship and continued support is greatly appreciated.

Rita Briner of Quilter's Station, Lee's Summit, MO. Your continued support is appreciated. You are even willing to drop what you are doing (was that lunch you were making for one of your workshops?) to look at what I just made.

Pat Worth at River Reader in Lexington. What would I do without you and your wonderful bookstore and the best place to get away from all the work I need to do.

Deb Rowden, my editor - again thanks for all you do. We make a good team, and it is a pleasure to work with you again.

Aaron Leimkuehler, my photographer - again your photography is the best and I am so glad you are a part of this team, I wouldn't want to do this without you.

Brian Grubb, my book designer, your work just pulls this all together. You understand just what I want and your vision is greatly appreciated.

Lon Eric Craven my illustrator, Donna di Natale my technical editor and Jo Ann Groves my production assistant - your magic makes this work, thanks.

My friends here in Lexington that continue to support me and ask how the book is coming, hand hold when necessary and even volunteer to come over with plastic tubs to drag out clutter and with dust cloths to dust to help me get ready for the photo shoot! Your willingness to help does not go unnoticed or unappreciated.

Most of all, thanks again to my family, I couldn't do this without your love and support. My girls Heather and Cassandra are always there for me, my hubby Harold who still steps around my projects. I hope you are up to 'peddling' my book as you did last time, the trucking business will never be the same.

To all of you, those I have had the pleasure to meet and those I have not yet met, thank you. Without your wonderful support of my design work and workshops, this would not be possible.

Dedication

I dedicate this book to my girls,
Heather and Cassandra.
You both amaze me and
I am so proud of you.

About the Author

I am still amazed that I get to work at what I have a passion for, and on top of that, I get to do another book. This time nature is the subject, something I love to observe. It inspires me.

I have had the opportunity to work with some of my favorite designers: Barb Adams and Alma Allen from Blackbird Designs; Renee Nannaman of Need'l Love Company; and Linda Brannock of Star Quilt Designs. I have been able to design for individuals as well. This year I had an amazing opportunity to design and make a liturgical stole for a friend that became an ordained Deacon in the Episcopal Church. This was a very special assignment: it was very satisfying to create something of importance and very humbling at the same time.

I often wonder if growing up in a military family and moving often influenced me. It may be we had to find ways to entertain ourselves. Now I get to live and work here in my town of Lexington, MO. It is quaint: full of wonderful people, history and great old homes. And there is an abundance of creative people here. I have given up my shop in the log house. I prefer to travel and teach and I could not keep a shop going if I was always gone. I still sell antiques at shows and design rugs and patterns but I don't have to leave home to do it. Now that seems like a perfect formula to me!

Maggie

My source for my inspiration is the same that has been used forever: leaves, flowers, birds, trees and so on. All have been depicted in artwork, quilts, needlework, rugs as well as any other art medium. So this is nothing really new, but to me there is something about the way it proceeds through each season, showing us something new or something we have waited a year to see again. It could be the first snowflake, purple violet or blooming dogwood - or when fields are fresh with wildflowers. Maybe it is when the leaves start to turn and we know we have made it through the hot summer - a sure sign the seasons are changing. A big orange pumpkin to the fresh evergreens and holly gathered around the holidays that signal we are at years' end.

last. Now anyone happening to look out their window as I gathered these leaves would have thought I was gathering up something more precious (such as money I had dropped). These beautiful little works of art were precious in their own right. I brought them home and pressed them between the pages of a book to dry and enjoy later. I also had a thing for acorns, big or small, green or black. I had to have them and would come home with my pockets filled with them, filling a bowl with my found treasure. Maybe I was a squirrel in another life.

My Thoughts on Nature

I am partial to the leaf, flower and bird part of nature (you could say the pretty side). I have had unfortunate encounters with the creepy-crawly and I even hate to say it - the slithering kind of nature - for I have had to deal with them in my house!

I love collecting bits of nature, leaves and nests and acorns. I have to tell you a little story: I used to walk my dog down the street and just a few houses down was the most wonderful sugar maple. It was the first tree in the neighborhood to change color. Now as I walked down past the tree there would be a beautiful orange leaf in the street which I immediately picked up. Well, a few steps further there was another, then another. I gathered each as they were more beautiful than the

Nature constantly gives us something to inspire us. It may be the color or the texture or even the smell. I am always happy to gather a roadside bouquet or a bundle of bare branches in a crock along with all the other bits of nature I lay out to enjoy.

Sometimes it is not only nature's season but it may be the light of day, night, rain or snow. I am not well versed in the science of nature but there is such beauty to be seen and great color and subjects to be inspired by. Just take a good long look at all that is around you. How could you not want to get out your wools or fabric and just make something?

A leaf, a sunbeam, a landscape
What is common to them all—
that perfectness and harmony,
is beauty.
— Nature

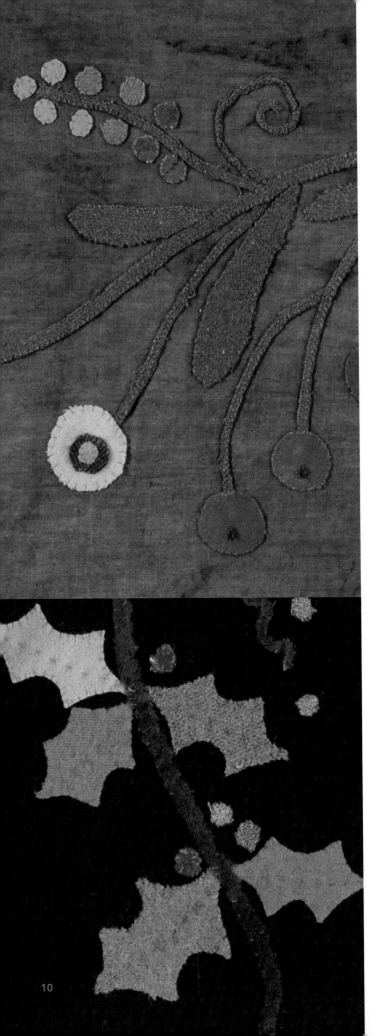

I am always asked what type of thread I use: it is Coats and Clarks 54A Summer Brown, regular sewing thread, I often refer to it as tan. I began using it years ago and it does just what I want it to so I continue. I am no way opposed to using any of the wonderful threads that are available. Use what you want.

What kind of stitch?

I use what I call a simple whip stitch, just stitching along the edge of the appliqué piece, up through the wool and down just off the edge into the background, then back up, continuing around the piece. If you want do a blanket stitch, please do. Mine was never very even so I don't do it (and it takes longer)!

Hand sewing supplies.

I usually refer to this as most everything I do is hand sewn. I prefer it, for me it is relaxing. A must is a needle of choice, as well as thread of choice. You'll also need scissors and pins and anything else that will make it easy for you.

Fabrics.

I use fabrics generally available at quilt shops or rug hooking studios. Occasionally I like to use antique fabrics, these can be found at antique shops and flea markets and I expect online and at auctions. Most quilt shops have wonderful reproduction fabrics: many also carry linen as well as velvets and wools. Regarding wools used in these projects, I must say that the washed and dyed wools will vary greatly at times due to the weave as well as the dye process, all wool will shrink when washed and even more so when dyed. Use the fabric requirements and measurements given for the project as guides. I always buy a little extra if in doubt.

Antiquing fabric.

I have often used tan Rit dye or teabags to gently age my fabric. There are "antiquing sprays" made from walnut crystals that are great to use and actually easier than dyeing. These are available at many quilt and needlework shops. If not available locally, look online under walnut crystals.

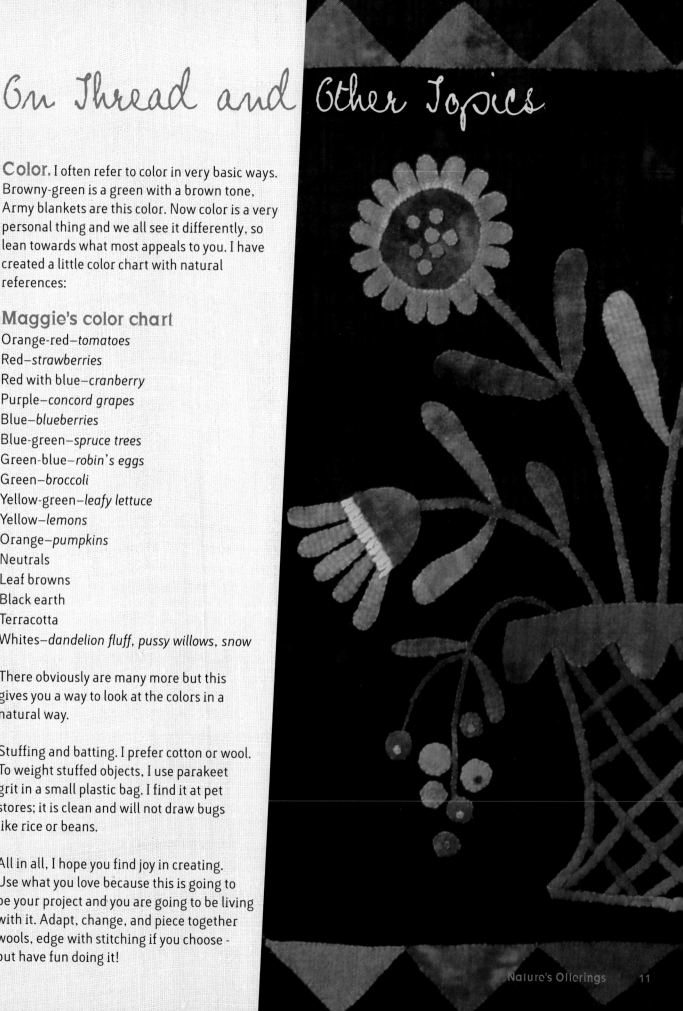

On Thread and Other Topics

Color. I often refer to color in very basic ways. Browny-green is a green with a brown tone, Army blankets are this color. Now color is a very personal thing and we all see it differently, so lean towards what most appeals to you. I have created a little color chart with natural references:

Maggie's color chart

Orange-red—*tomatoes*
Red—*strawberries*
Red with blue—*cranberry*
Purple—*concord grapes*
Blue—*blueberries*
Blue-green—*spruce trees*
Green-blue—*robin's eggs*
Green—*broccoli*
Yellow-green—*leafy lettuce*
Yellow—*lemons*
Orange—*pumpkins*
Neutrals
Leaf browns
Black earth
Terracotta
Whites—*dandelion fluff, pussy willows, snow*

There obviously are many more but this gives you a way to look at the colors in a natural way.

Stuffing and batting. I prefer cotton or wool. To weight stuffed objects, I use parakeet grit in a small plastic bag. I find it at pet stores; it is clean and will not draw bugs like rice or beans.

All in all, I hope you find joy in creating. Use what you love because this is going to be your project and you are going to be living with it. Adapt, change, and piece together wools, edge with stitching if you choose - but have fun doing it!

*There is no season such
delight can bring
As summer, Autumn, winter
and the spring."*
*~ Wm Browne
1591-1645*

The projects in this book are inspired by nature. As the year progresses, each season has a distinct look. I wanted to take you through the year as I see it. My projects are grouped by seasons - but each could be adapted to fit others as well.

The projects in this book

We enjoy all four seasons here in the Midwest. I know some of you do not have the weather changes we have and may be lucky because as I write this, we have had terrible storms and high humidity, but this is the Midwest - what would you expect? I hope you will enjoy this journey through the year with me.

Spring

Spring comes early in some places and the violets on the cute little lavender pincushions could be seen in most yards. I have two versions of this little pillow. What spring could not have a couple of silly rabbits? I have included two here: one is made of dyed grey velvet and the other of natural linen. Either would be fun to have sitting by a pot of pansies or herbs. Spring also brings a lot of birds nesting in our trees, so I have made a small round hooked chair pad of a nest with three blue eggs. This could become a pillow top as well.

To start off the year, our first project is a 'white on white' bed cover that represents the cold snowy weather we often begin the year with. The bed cover is wool appliqué on old white linen. It's a wonderful wintery garden and would be fabulous taken one step further with quilting. Next, as winter winds down, we have that period of browns. There is no longer snow, but it's too early for even the smallest of buds to appear. The Primitive Flower Basket Hooked Rug fills this seasonal bill, a great folky rug done all in neutrals. It would be perfect anywhere, any season. I used a wide wool strip and this worked up quickly.

are inspired by NATURE

Summer

Summer quickly arrives and my Tropicals Under Glass wool appliqué table rug reminded me of how fast plants will send out new leaves and tendrils especially if they are given the protection of a glass cloche used to protect it from late frosts. My papercut Bee Skep in the Garden is reminiscent of a warm day. Watching the bees move among the flowers and herbs, I think I can even smell the sweet scent of the garden. The fruit basket appliqué is made primarily in cottons - inspired by the old Theorem pictures where baskets of fruit were stenciled onto velvet. This project can be framed or made into a pillow or just left as is as I did mine. Summer brings fresh ripe fruit - something to remember long into the winter.

Summer's Bounty can be celebrated with oversized veggies: a beet with wonderful wired leaves and a big velvet carrot with wiry greens growing out the top. Display them in a big old wood bowl or a wire basket - each can also be useful as a folk art pincushion. I have included a small velvet tomato, representative of traditional tomato pincushions. Make up a bunch of these in varied fabrics and red colors and fill an old glass apothecary jar, or just set them out with the other veggies.

On a cold day later in the year, you will appreciate the warmth of the Wildflowers of Summer Wool Bed Cover. The wildflowers are appliquéd and strewn around the border, as well as in a big basket in the center.

Fall

Fall brings a group of 'Camp Projects'. These are quick and easy items to make, something you might like to do on a warm fall afternoon. There is one project I call a camp leaf picture. It is a little bit of appliqué, a few twigs and a fall verse that I like - something to hang up to remind you of this season and of 'camp'. There are two little notebooks/journals to make with a little fabric, brown paper and some twigs as well, perfect for recording your nature observations. An Acorn and Leaf Needlekeep Pincushion is quick and would make a sweet gift for a sewing friend. You will also make a single acorn with paper leaves: perfect to use as an ornament or hanging by itself from a knob of your favorite cupboard.

I also added a Gourd Make-Do Pincushion. I had the top part of a gourd and made a fabric bottom for it so it now has a pear shape. There are lots of gourds out there in the fall, you will need a tool to cut off the top portion of the gourd. This is an example where I need to make something out of a leftover.

The 1870 Urn Table Runner is a nice reminder of the fall: leaves and flower placed in a crock to enjoy the end of the season. Go out and gather what is nearby and be pleased with a free bouquet for your table.

Pears seem to ripen in the fall so I have made some Autumn Pears. One large pear would be suited well enough along with your summer veggies. It has a sculptural quality so it can also stand alone: set it on a small pedestal as a piece of folk art. Of course it can also work as a pincushion. The Sewing Pear Make-Do even has a button added to hold a loop of ribbon that has been threaded through the scissors, keeping them at hand for your next sewing project.

Fall is not complete without a big orange pumpkin. The Punkin stool cover I made shows one made with several dark rusty orange wools. The cover is just tied in place. This design could be adapted for a different sized stool, or even made into a pillow. I still see twig stools out there in antique shops and antique shows.

Winter

Winter begins to approach as the year comes to a close. I have included a couple of holly projects that could decorate your winter table or be perfect for Christmas. One is wool appliqué on wool: it would not be difficult to double in size. I've also made two small embroidery holly branches. I like them left as they are but if you prefer to have a more finished look just turn a small hem all around. These small pieces are perfect to 'lay about' just about anywhere you wish. The embroidery pattern could be used on a table cloth or runner, just about anything. My final project is a Paper Dove made from a manila folder and some script paper I found and photocopied. Of course the scrapbook shops have many wonderful papers to use. These doves are dimensional and love to fly from your tree or green swags – even from a light fixture. If you wanted, you could cut a tiny heart and hang it from its beak, a perfect Valentine for February.

I hope you will try these projects, they are meant to be fun and even functional, but not too serious. Use materials that are available. I still do not go to auctions or online to shop, I just buy fabric and material I like to use, knowing eventually I will use them, contrary to my hubby's advice, "If it hasn't been used in a year, throw it out!" How unkind is that?

To be creative I have to be surrounded with things I might use, my stash not only has wools and fabric but old papers, ribbons, yarn and oh yes, spirea branches. Who knew? There are also leaves, acorns, abandoned bird nests, shards of hatched bird eggs, even an empty wasp nest. I love to gather these things around; they are little treasures to me that nature has provided.

So go through my book and pick out something you want to make. Enjoy yourself and as my favorite author says:

Live each season as it passes, Breathe the air, drink the drink, taste the fruit and resign yourself to the influences of each.

~ Henry David Thoreau

Winter's Garden Bed Cover
48" x 60"

As the New Year begins at my home in Missouri, winter is usually well on its way. We will usually have at least one snow fall where the snowflakes are huge and they softly stack up on everything: tree limbs, fence rails, even bird baths and planters left out from last summer. The world seems isolated from everything else: it's quiet and calm, a nice change after the holidays with all the glitz and glitter and hectic schedules. Whether I get snow or not, I prefer to change my surroundings by bringing out my white wool blankets, linens, old ironstone, trading those colorful things for the cool calm of whites. I look forward to regrouping for the year, enjoying a good book and something to stitch or a rug to hook. This calm usually only lasts a few weeks - enough to recoup a little energy for the rest of the year.

For this bedcover, I used on old linen sheet I found but new linen, wool or even a good flannel would work well also. The design is hand appliquéd using three different white wools and a border with corner blocks. I hand appliquéd but had to actually bring out my sewing machine to join the borders.

Materials needed

2 1/2 yards natural or antique white linen

Thin unbleached cotton batting (I use Hobbs), twin size 72" x 96"

3 yards cotton fabric for backing

White wools for the appliqué:

Wool A (the lightest) 24" x 45"

Wool B (medium) 12" x 30"

Wool C (darkest) 20" x 24"

Matching off-white thread

Hand sewing supplies

Sewing machine

The North wind doth blow
And we shall have snow.

Assembly

The pattern pieces tell which wool to use. The center section measures 33" x 45". Use the diagram on page 19 to place the appliqué. The urn is centered along the bottom edge with the rim added to sit just along top of it. The vines are all cut from wool A: 1/2" by the length shown on the diagram. The small stems and vine tendrils need to be less than 1/4" and taper to a point on the end so they curve and turn.

If your fabric is lightweight, add the cotton batting to stabilize while you stitch. I actually used matching thread in this project instead of the tan thread I usually use. Once you have the center design complete, cut 4 - 9" blocks, 2 pieces 9" x 45", and 2 pieces 9" x 33". Cut batting the same size (if you are using it). Here is where I had to use my sewing machine due to the batting layer. Using a 1/2" seam, sew the 45" sides first, sew the corner blocks to the 33" lengths and sew them to the bedcover. I made a scalloped edging for the borders by cutting strips of wool 'A' to fit along the outer edge of the center section x 2 1/2" wide (see diagram on page 19). The top and bottom strips need to be cut into 16 sections (about 2" each). Leaving one e dge straight, curve the top of each section to form the scallops. Do the same for the side borders, making at least 21 sections, doing the same as before. Stitch these scallops in place, including the scalloped edge. The corner blocks have 2 leaves and a curly tendril, the center of the top border has the year and is bordered by 2 leaves.

Winter's Garden

stem and tendril lengths
and placement

To finish this bedcover, I pieced cotton fabric and stitched it 'pillowcase' fashion on 3 sides, right sides together, turned right side out and hand stitched the fourth side. I did a running stitch around the outer edge. This could be finished as you wish. If you are a quilter, I think it would be fabulous quilted with a binding of linen. Either way, it is a wonderful bedcover.

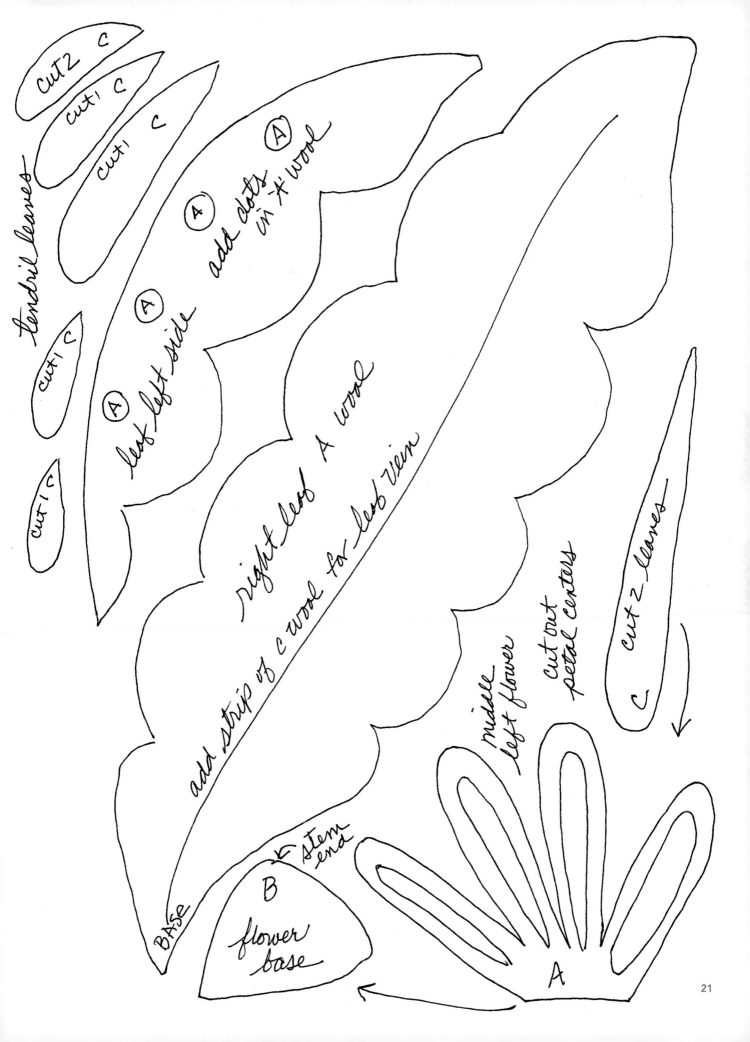

Cut 2 C

Cut 1 C

Cut 1 C

tendril leaves

Cut 1 C

Cut 1 C

Ⓐ

Ⓐ

Ⓐ add dots
in "A" wool

Ⓐ leaf left side

right leaf A wool

add strip of C wool for leaf vein

middle
left flower

cut out
petal centers

C cut 2 leaves

BASE

B ← stem
end

flower
base

A

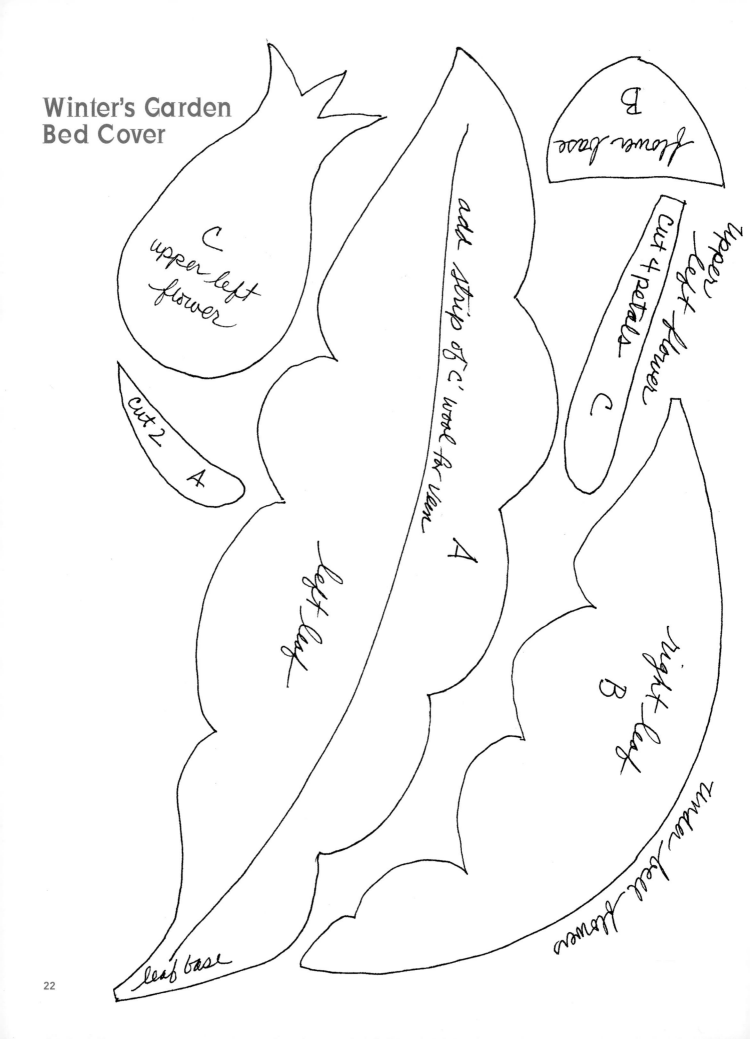

C
upper left
flower

cut 2   A

add strip of 'c' wool for vein   A

left leaf

B
flower base

cut 4 petals   C

upper left flower

right leaf
B

under leaf flower

leaf base

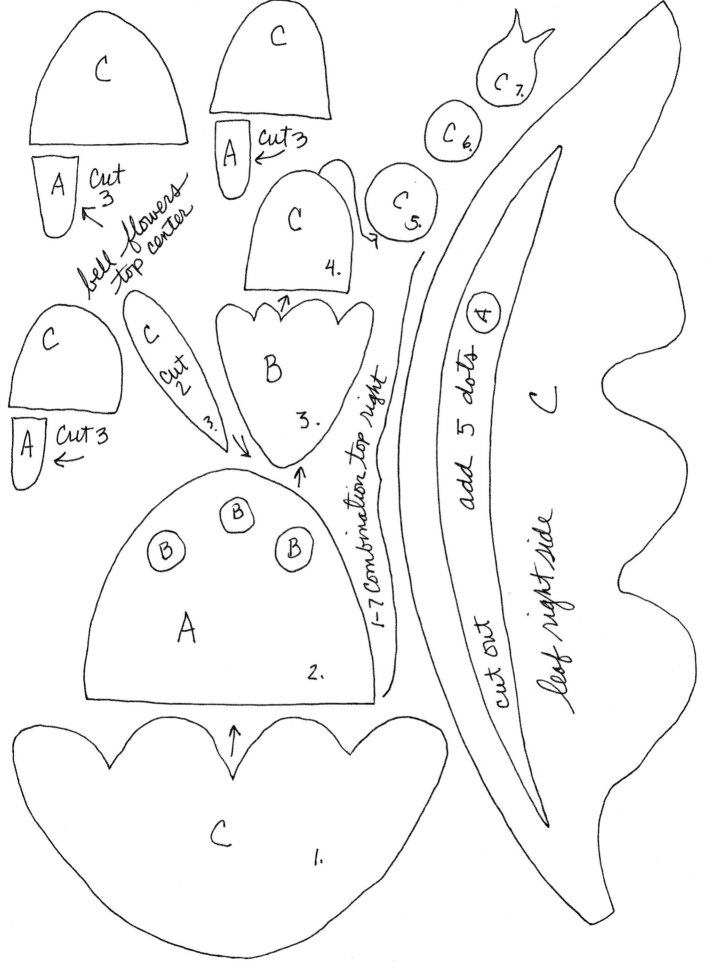

C

C

A Cut 3

A Cut 3

bell flowers top center

C

A Cut 3

C 7.

C 6.

C 5.

C 4.

C Cut 2 3.

B 3.

1-7 Combination top right

B

B

B

A

2.

add 5 dots A

cut out

C

leaf right side

C 1.

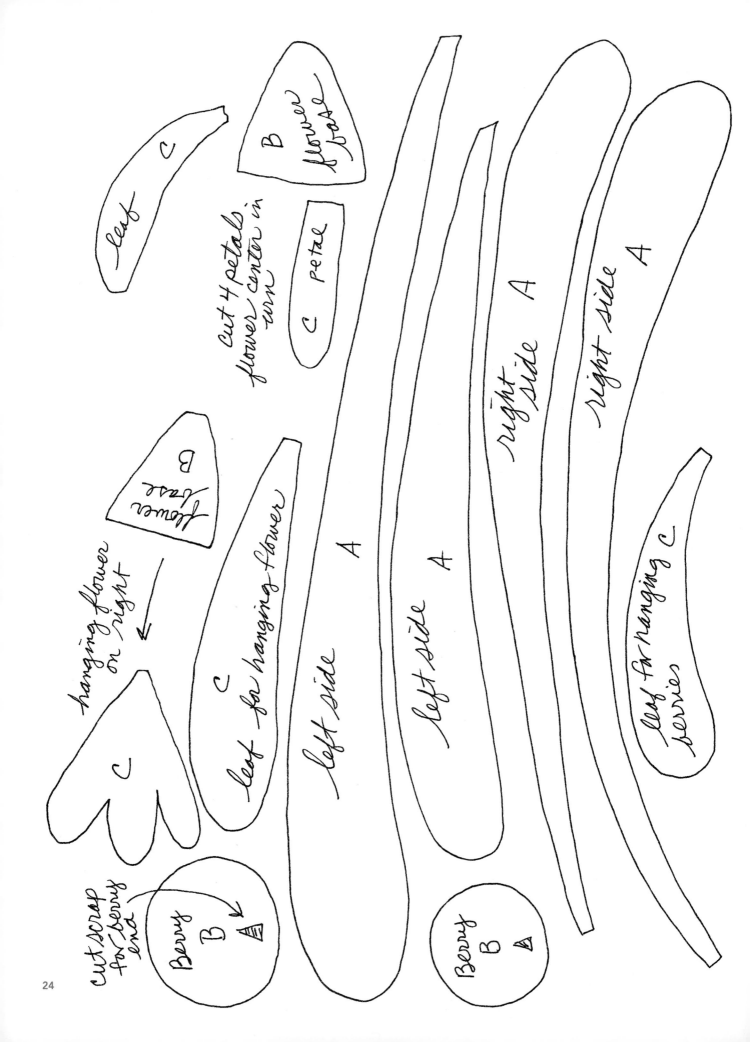

leaf
C

B
flower base

cut 4 petals
flower center in
urn

C petal

B
flower base

hanging flower
on right

C
leaf for hanging flower

right side   A

right side   A

left side   A

left side   A

leaf for hanging C
berries

C

cut scrap
for berry
end

Berry
B
A

Berry
B
A

Winter's Garden
Bed Cover

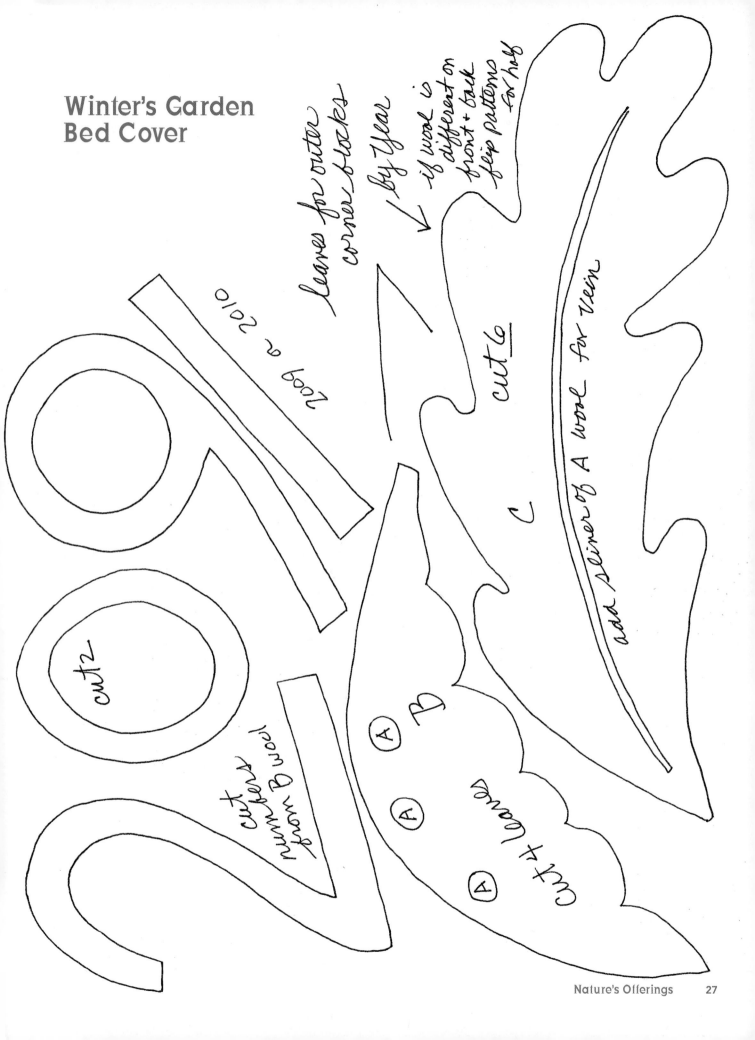

leaves for outer corner blocks

by Year

2009 ~ 2010

if wool is different on front + back skip patterns for hob

cut 6

C

add slivers of A wool for vein

cut 2

B

A

A

cut numbers from B wool

Cut 1 each

A

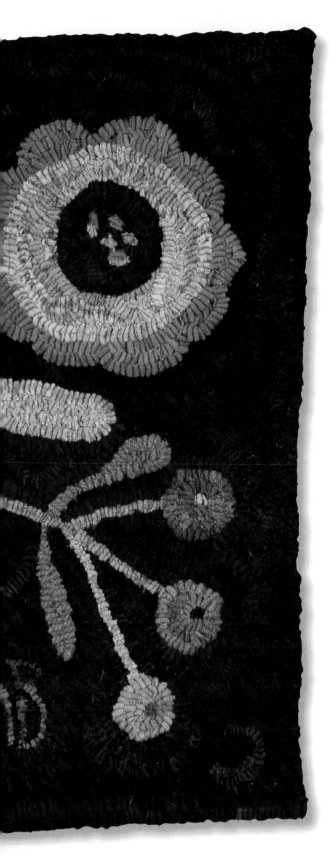

Primitive Flower Basket Hooked Rug
33" x 24"

This primitive rug was fun to make and hooked quickly. The neutral colors remind me of the trees outside in late winter just waiting for that spring color to arrive. Dreary as that might seem, I love these colors. Of course, you can choose any color you want to hook it with.

Since hooking style varies from person to person, my wool requirements are just suggestions. I use a wide strip but hook low, someone hooking higher would use more wool. My strips are torn double the width I want then I cut in two lengthwise. This gives the rug a more primitive look, adding variation to the texture.

Fabric requirements

41" x 32" Monks cloth or linen (design area is 33" x 24")
Assorted wools of each color group
Fat quarter light brown
1/2 yard dark brown
3/4 yard light grey/neutral
Fat quarter pumpkiny tan
1 1/2 yards dark browny black
Note: wool fat quarters measure approximately 17" x 28".

Assembly

Hook as you desire. Be sure to include initials and a date of choice, finishing off the rug as you choose. I have learned there are many ways to do this - do what works for you. I am not too good at finishing!
Note: patterns for this rug are on pages 98-107.

Primitive Flower Basket Maggie Bonanomi

Tropicals Under Glass
40" x 24" Wool Appliqué Table Rug

This rug was originally designed for a charity auction in a completely different color. I thought this would be a good nature project: the flowers look like they are growing before your eyes, like plants seem to do after the spring rains and after the heat of summer has kicked in. When I was finished with this piece, it looked to me like the tropical plant was under a glass cloche, so that is how it got its name. You can use this on a table, sofa back, on the wall, or as a hearth rug.

Materials needed

40" x 24" antique black wool (or assorted black wool pieced together to make that size) for background

1/4 yard medium brown wool for urn and edging

4" x 28" browny green wool for stems and tendrils

10" x 13" browny green wool for leaves, urn edging, flower bases

10" x 11" medium green wool for leaves and flower bases

Assorted soft yellow gold wool totaling 20" x 4" for flower petals

Cotton fabric for backing

Assembly

Prepare the black background by following the diagram on page 32 to cut half circle.

Refer to the diagram for tendril and stem lengths and placement as well as leaf placement.

First place the urn centered about 1" above bottom edge, cut out stems. They are 1/4" by the length noted on the diagram. Tendrils are cut with the ends tapering to a point so they curl nicely. I suggest you join together leaf parts first, then position them on the background. Stitch all in place with a simple whip stitch.

For the edging, measure across the bottom and up around the outer edge of the background. You need enough 1 1/2" strips to go around. Clip at about 3/4" intervals along one edge, leaving about 1/8" uncut along the bottom edge (see diagram). Just eyeball this – it need not be exact. Go back and round off the top edges into scallop shapes.

The uncut edge of the edging goes under the outer edge of your mat, whip stitch it in place. Be sure to cut and add some initials or a date (see page 110-111 for an alphabet and page 111 for numerals).

Finish by adding the backing, turning under the raw edges and stitching in place.

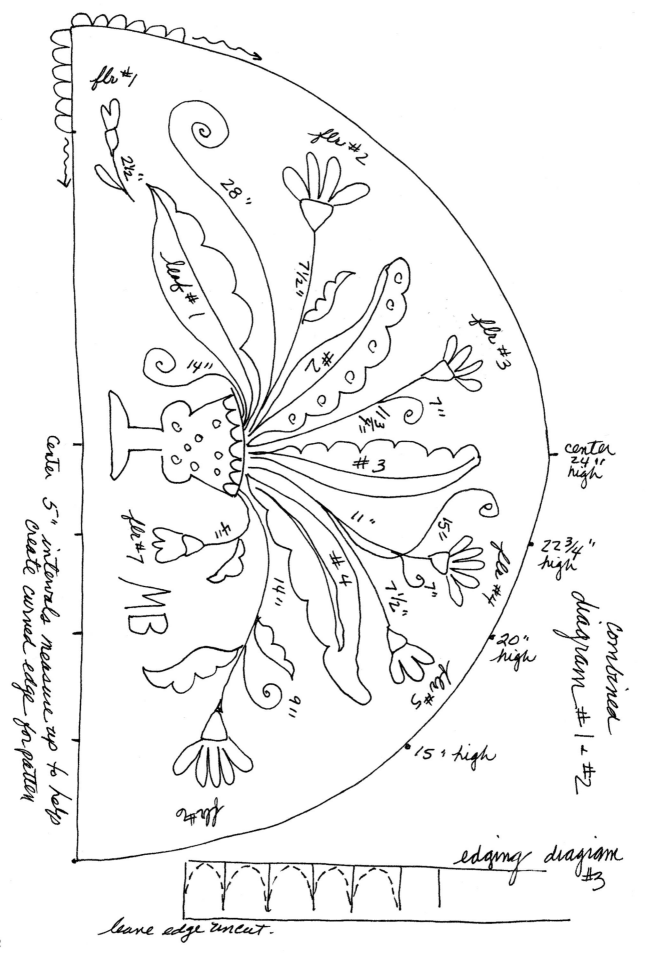

flr #1

2½"

28"

flr #2

7½"

leaf #1

14"

#2

flr #3

13½"

7"

#3

11"

#4

14"

#4

flr #7

MB

9"

flr #6

flr #5

7½"

7"

15½"

flr #4

center
24" high

22¾"
high

20"
high

15" high

combined diagram #1 + #2

center   5" intervals measure up to help
create curved edge for pattern

edging diagram
#3

leave edge uncut.

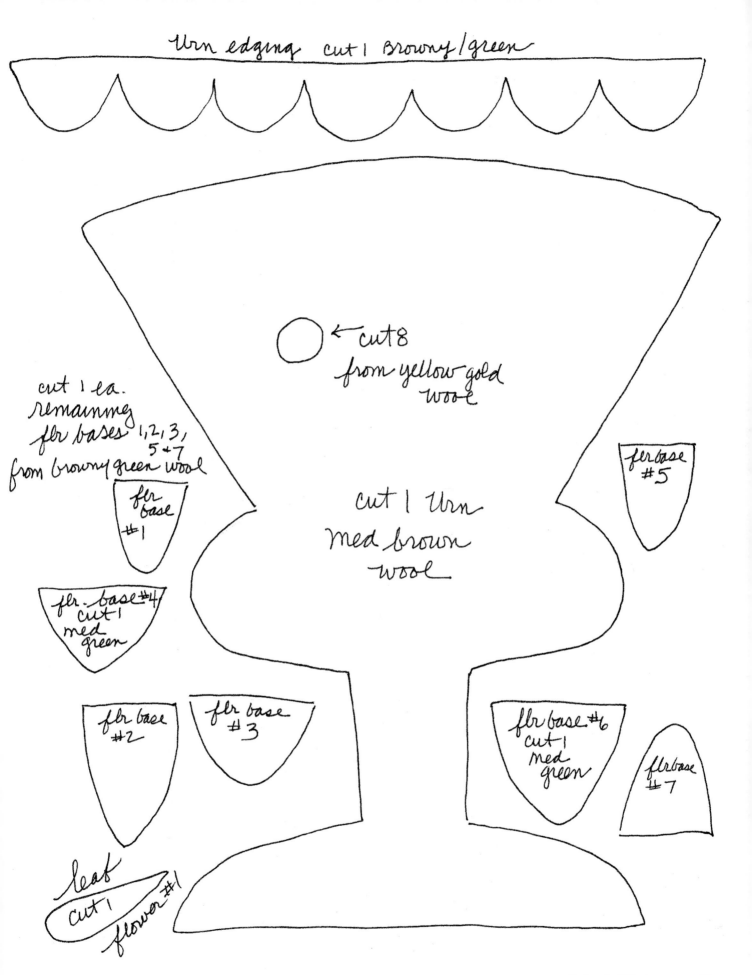

Urn edging cut 1 Browny/green

← cut 8
from yellow gold
wool

cut 1 ea.
remaining
flr bases 1,2,3,
5+7
from browny green wool

flr base #5

cut 1 Urn
med brown
wool

flr base #1

flr. base #4
cut 1
med
green

flr base #2

flr base #3

flr base #6
cut 1
med
green

flrbase #7

leaf
cut 1
flower #1

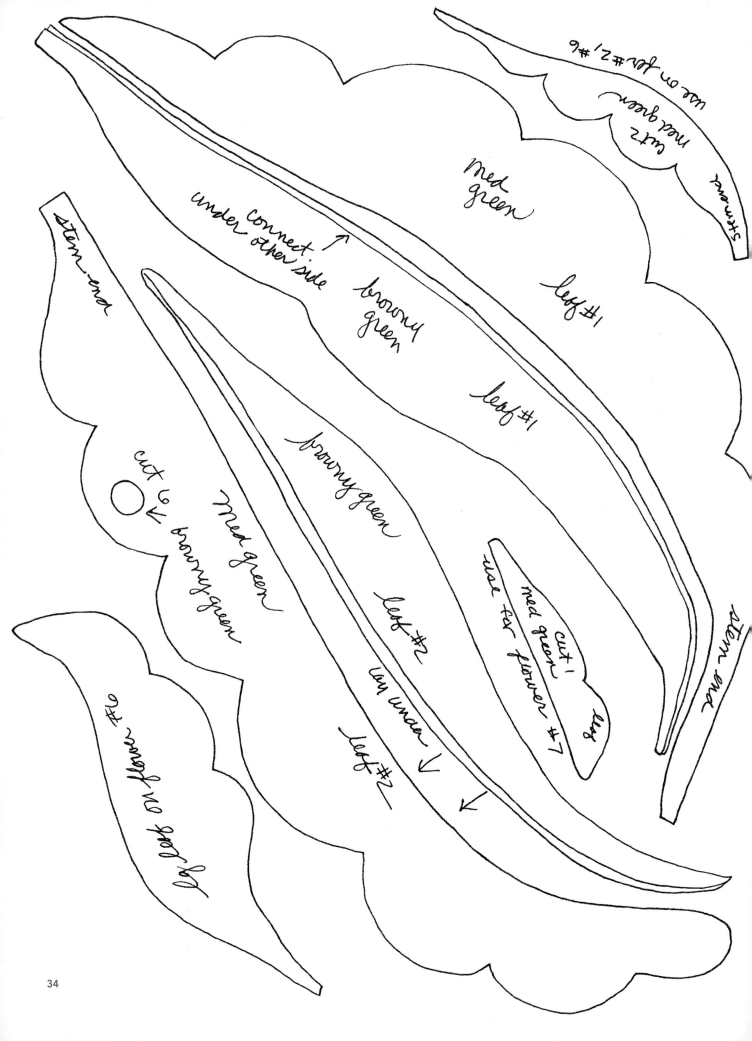

Med
green

leaf #1

cut 2
med green
use on leaf #2, #6

Stem end

Connect
under other side

browny
green

leaf #1

stem end

browny green

med green
browny green

cut 6

leaf #2

lay under

leaf #2

cut 1
med green
use for flower #7

leag

stem end

leaf or flower #6

34

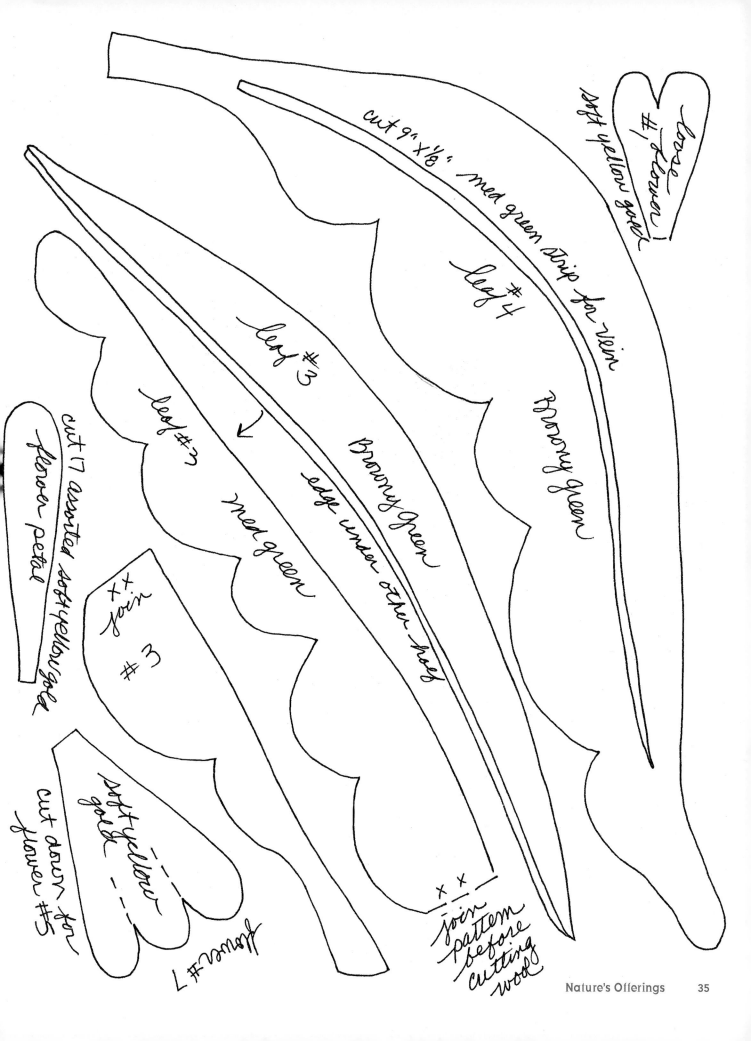

cut 9" x ⅛" med green strip for vein

leaf #4

Browny green

leaf #3

Browny green

edge under other hals

leaf #2

med green

XX
join
#3

cut 17 assorted soft yellow gold
flower petal

soft yellow
gold

flower #1

cut down for
flower #5

x x
join
pattern
before
cutting
wood

leave
flower
#1

soft yellow gold

Sweet Violets

4" x 5" Pillows

Another symbol of early spring are the violets that grow wild in the woods and yards.
I made this project two ways: one a lavender-filled linen pillow, the other a wool pillow.
For the linen version I used over-dyed linen, lightly tea-stained (or a light solution of water
and Rit tan dye). The leaves are scraps of brownish green linen, stems are green chenille
yarn, and plum silk ribbon for the blossoms.

Wool pillow

Materials needed

6" x 5 1/4" antique white wool

1 1/2" x 4" dark violet wool for petals

8" x 2" Army green wool for leaves and stems

6" x 5 1/4" cotton or wool for backing

4 pearl buttons

Tan thread or color of your choice

Cotton stuffing

Assembly

Cut out pattern pieces and refer to the photo on the next page for placement – stitch in place. The stems are thin strips of wool 4" x 1/8". The curly stem is 7" cut very narrow and couch stitched in place. Appliqué in place with a simple whip stitch, add buttons on curly stem.

Stitch together the front and back, right sides together, on 3 sides. Turn right side out, stuff with cotton stuffing, and stitch closed.

Either of these little pillows could be a pincushion, the lavender one would be a lovely sachet for a drawer or closet but it is too cute to hide away.

Assembly

Refer to the photo for placement of pattern pieces. Appliqué the leaves in place, couch stitch the chenille for stems. Cut the ribbon into 7 - 1 1/4" pieces. Turn under raw edge of ribbon for outer edge of petal and stitch down. Turn under and gather edge to become petal center, stitch in place. Add a small snip of green chenille for the flower center. The bent flower has just 2 petals. Add 4 pearl buttons as 'seeds' on the curled stem.

Stitch front and back, right sides together, on three sides. Turn right side out. Stuff a small bit of stuffing into the corners, fill firmly with lavender buds. Add a bit of stuffing to the top edge and stitch closed.

Linen Pillow

Materials needed

6" x 5 1/4" linen or cotton

6" x 5 1/4" cotton or velvet backing

3" square of greenish brown linen or cotton for leaves

15" green chenille yarn for stems

9" plum silk ribbon for flower petals

Tan thread (or matching color)

Four pearl buttons

2.5 oz. loose lavender buds

Small bit of cotton stuffing

Hand sewing supplies

cut 1 army green wool leaf

cut 7 dk violet wool petals

cut 1 army green blossom end (bent flower)

cut 1 army green wool leaf

cut 1 army green wool leaf

for cotton or linen leaves add seam allow

Silly Rabbit

About 8 1/2" tall

Note: this is not designed as a child's toy!

Rabbits seem to be another sign of spring. This silly rabbit is easy to make and can be made in multiples. I like to have him sitting on a table among spring veggie and herb plant starts or a pot of pansies.

I used grey velvet for one rabbit and made another one of old linen (easily found in the form of old tea towels). The Silly Rabbit would also be wonderful in wool, homespun or calico.

Materials needed

15" x 12" linen or velvet, grey or natural (or you choose) for rabbit body

3" wool square (match color to above choice) for rabbit bottom

3" x 5" cotton scrap for inner ears

One 12" chenille stem for arms

12" white or tan embroidery floss or string for whiskers and nose

2 black seed beads or 2 black topped straight pins or black floss for French knots for eyes

Box of birdcage gravel and grit for weight

Plastic baggie and twist tie or tape

Hand sewing supplies

Thread

Embroidery needle for whiskers and nose

Assembly

Cut out the pattern pieces (see page 40). Stitch the rabbit body from the neck around the head and down the back, then add the front piece. Clip curves, turn right side out, stuff firmly about 3/4 full. Fill the plastic baggie with grit (about the size of a good lemon), twist and tape closed and place in the bottom of rabbit with a bit of stuffing to smooth the appearance. Gather stitch the bottom edge, stuff firmly, gather up just enough to attach the wool bottom, tie off thread. Stitch wool circle in place to cover the base.

Ears: stitch fabric and linen/velvet together (see diagram #1 on page 41). Stitch up one side around the tip, then down about 1/2". Turn the ear right side out, turn under raw edges and continue to stitch down ear. Turn in the raw bottom edge. Stitch to rabbit head (these are droopy ears).

Arms: cut the chenille stem in half. Bend down one end (for each arm) so length is 4 1/4", wrap lightly in stuffing. Fold the fabric for the arm, stitch around one end (see diagram #2 on page 41). Turn right side out, insert the bent end into the end just stitched. Turn in raw edges and stitch down, leaving about 1 1/2" unstitched. Lay this end opened, trim as shown (see diagram #3 on page 41), attach the arm along the shoulder mark on the pattern. Secure the arms.

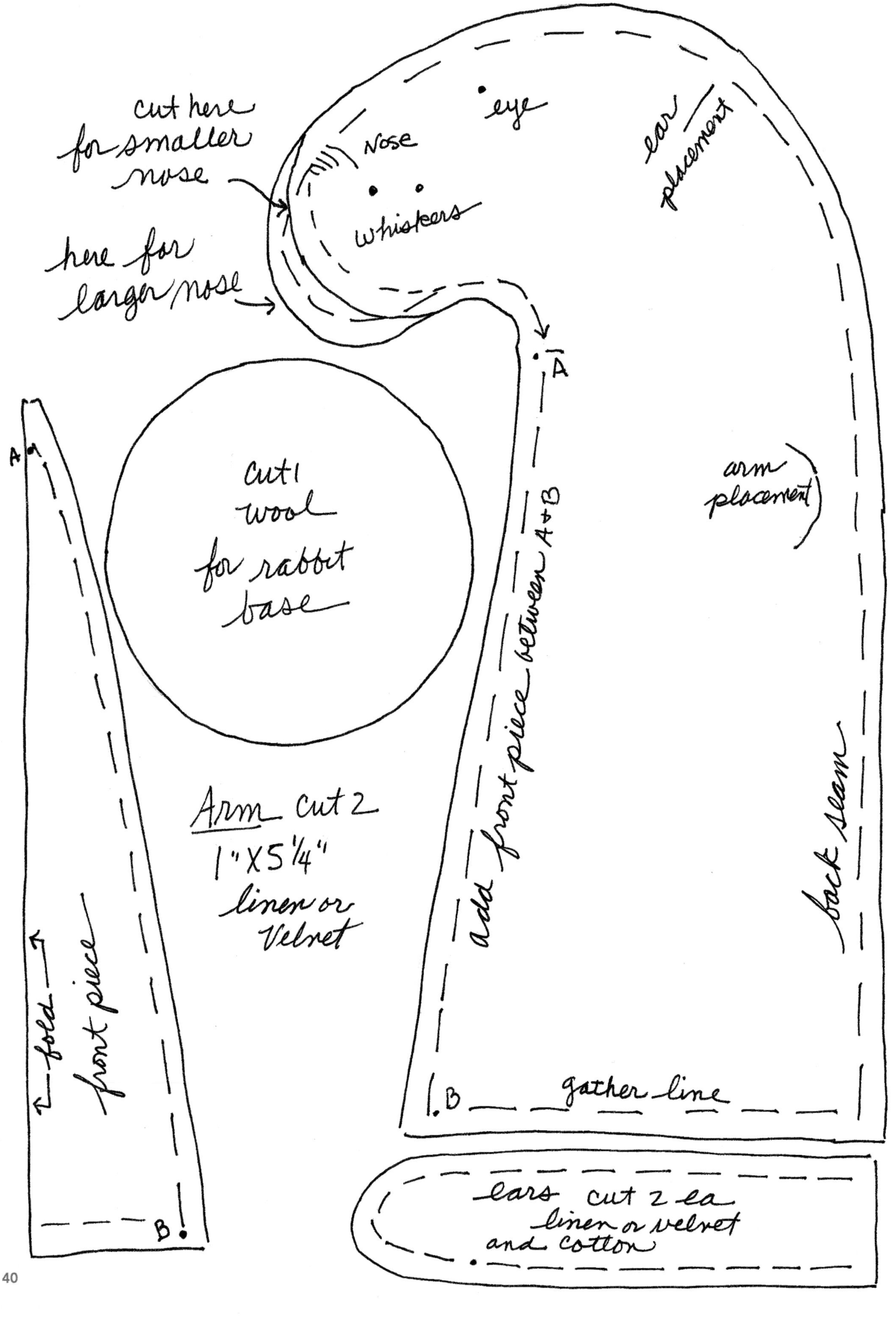

cut here
for smaller
nose

here for
larger nose

Nose   · eye

whiskers

ear placement

cut 1
wool
for rabbit
base

A

A

arm placement

add front piece between A + B

Arm cut 2
1" X 5¼"
linen or
velvet

fold

front piece

back seam

B

gather line

B

ears cut 2 ea
linen or velvet
and cotton

ear
diagram #1

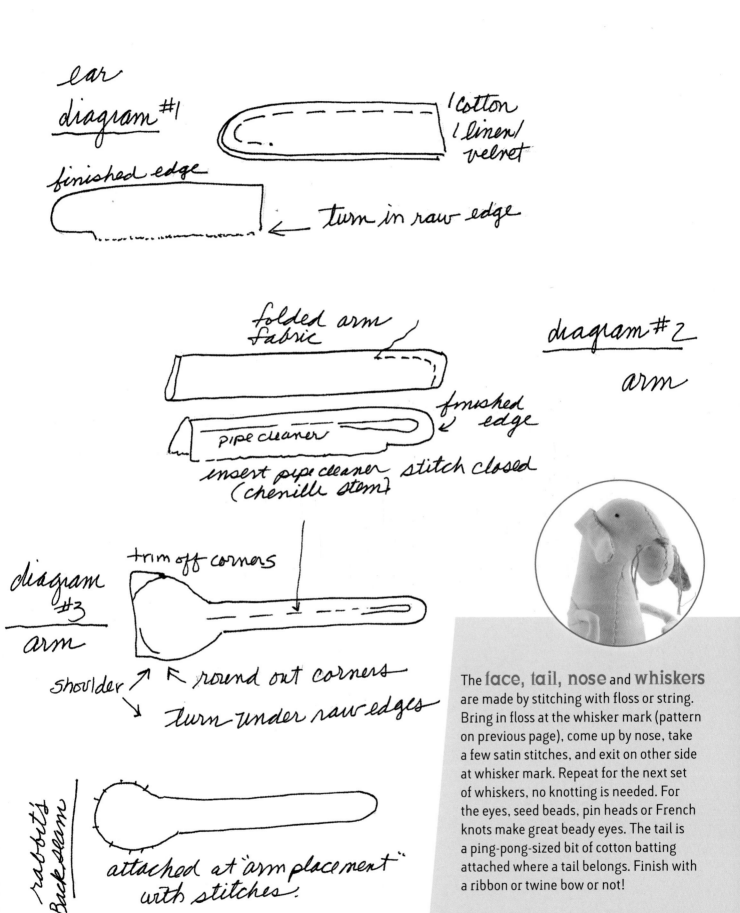

cotton
linen/
velvet

finished edge

← turn in raw edge

folded arm
fabric

diagram #2
arm

finished
edge

pipe cleaner

insert pipe cleaner (chenille stem) stitch closed

diagram
#3
arm

trim off corners

shoulder ↗ ← round out corners
↘ turn under raw edges

rabbit's
Back seam

attached at "arm placement"
with stitches.

The **face, tail, nose** and **whiskers** are made by stitching with floss or string. Bring in floss at the whisker mark (pattern on previous page), come up by nose, take a few satin stitches, and exit on other side at whisker mark. Repeat for the next set of whiskers, no knotting is needed. For the eyes, seed beads, pin heads or French knots make great beady eyes. The tail is a ping-pong-sized bit of cotton batting attached where a tail belongs. Finish with a ribbon or twine bow or not!

Careful, these can multiply easily!

Bird Nest
Hooked Chair Pad
11" circular

A nest of blue eggs surely signals spring! These wonderful little structures made of grass and twigs amaze me. How does the bird get the first few twigs to stay put until she can weave together the remaining pieces? These little nests are often lined with downy grasses and become a secure little home until the hatched birdies fly away! I have often collected the remains of the egg shell that has blown out of the nest after the little birds have hatched. The robin's egg blue ones are just beautiful. These little shards of nature's own color pallet would be hard to replicate.

This design is a nest setting on a small branch with three blue eggs. I made mine into a chair pad but would be great finished as a pillow.

Materials needed

18" Monks cloth or linen

The wool requirements are approximate, as each person hooks differently:

3 pieces blue wool, 12" x 2" each, for eggs and edging

12" x 2" black or dark brown wool for nest center

12" x 4" medium brown wool for nest base

5 assorted dark tan wools, a few strips each, for twigs on nest

12" x 2" medium brown wool for outer edge of mat

12" x 2" taupe/grey wool for branch

12" x 25" assorted green wools for leaves and background

Assembly

Hook the chair pad, finishing by pulling up a thin strip of the blue wools along the inner edge of your outer border. I finished my chair pad by trimming away the excess foundation fabric, leaving about 1 1/2" to turn under and stitch down. Cover this with twill tape stitched along outer edge of last row of hooking...or finish as you please.

Note: patterns for this rug are on pages 108-109.

Wildflowers of Summer Wool Bed Cover

58" square

This comfy appliquéd wool bed cover reminded me of the wildflowers growing in late summer.

It consists of a center section with a basket of wildflowers, surrounded by a 3" border of triangles, and an outer 10" border with vines running up and around the outside with leaves, flowers and berries. The vines twine thru the year appliquéd at the top and finally, the outer edge has more triangles, a wool version of prairie points.

The wools I used were from Blackberry Primitives, they are all hand dyed and vary from piece to piece. I also used several varied pieces of wool in most colors to add interest. The size of a fat half yard of wool is approximately 17" x 56", a fat quarter yard is approximately 17" x 28" in some cases it will be easier to just buy fat quarters or larger. Different weaves of wool will shrink differently which is why they are approximate. Measurement of wool is after it has been washed and dyed.

Materials needed

2 yards antique black wool for bedcover background (width 60")

1 yard assorted browny greens wools for vines, stems, leaves, and triangles

Fat quarter brown sugar (warm medium brown) wool for basket and triangles

Fat quarter rusty brown wool for berries and triangles

Fat quarter green with blue-green wool for leaves, berries, and triangles

12" x 4" blue-green wool for flowers, berries, and triangles

7" x 16" smokey grey wool for sunflower centers

18" x 7" mustard wool for sunflower petals, berries, and small flowers

6" square warm antique white wool for flower base and fringe

3" x 5" limey green or maybe substitute a browny green wool scrap for petal edge of flowers

Tan thread, needle

Lots of pins, scissors etc.

60" square cotton or ticking for backing

Assembly

The center section is 32" square:
you can piece this if desired. Cut out the basket rim and 30" of 1/2" strips of brown sugar wool. Refer to the diagram on page 47 to make basket outline, then add the crossed strips. I actually wove them "over and under" once they were laid out. You may want to go ahead and stitch them down, leaving the top edge of the basket unstitched for now so you can insert the stems next. The stems are 1/2" browny green wool, the hanging berry branch and viney tendril are 1/4" each – refer to the diagram for the lengths. Using the patterns and the color information on them, cut out the flowers, berries, and leaves. Pin in place and stitch down.

Next, add a 3" border all around the center section. Cut 2 - 3" antique black wool strips 32" and 2 - 38". Wool is very stretchy and even though I measured, I ended up adding pieces to get the correct length at times, maybe only on one side. When you attach the borders, overlap maybe 1/4" and stitch down with a simple whip stitch. The triangle pattern is on page 51: they are cut from assorted wools: browny green, bluegreens, browns, etc. There are 3 sizes of the triangle - use them randomly and place 6 on each side. These are appliquéd along the edge of the center block in the 3" strip.

The outer border is 10" wide. You
need 2 - 10" x 38" and 2 - 10" x 58" pieces of antique black wool: you can piece these to get the length you want. The measurements for the vines and tendrils that run through the border are shown on the diagram on page 47. The pattern pieces contain information about the leaves - cut these out of assorted greens. Refer to the diagram on page 47 for leaf and flower placement. The tendrils should taper at the end. I actually laid out the vine and added leaves and flowers as I moved along the vines, stitching as I went.

The year 2009 at the top has a tendril weaving through the numbers (see diagram).

For the outer edging, I used assorted wools (greens, rust, mustard, greeny blue, brown sugar)... Refer to the diagram to cut these outer triangles: cut several at a time of one color in a strip, leaving 1/2" uncut along the bottom edge. When they are separated, you will have 1/2" to put under the edge of the border to stitch down. You need 12 triangles per side - you may need to adjust the triangle size to fit.

Once you have finished the bedcover you may want to add backing for a finished look. Depending on the width of your backing fabric you may need to piece it together. I turned in 1/2" along the outer edge of the bedcover and just whip stitched it to the backing. You may want to stitch around the sections to hold the backing to the front. Now you have a great wool cover to curl up with when you are remembering warmer days.

detail of vine thru 'year'

vine and stem lengths

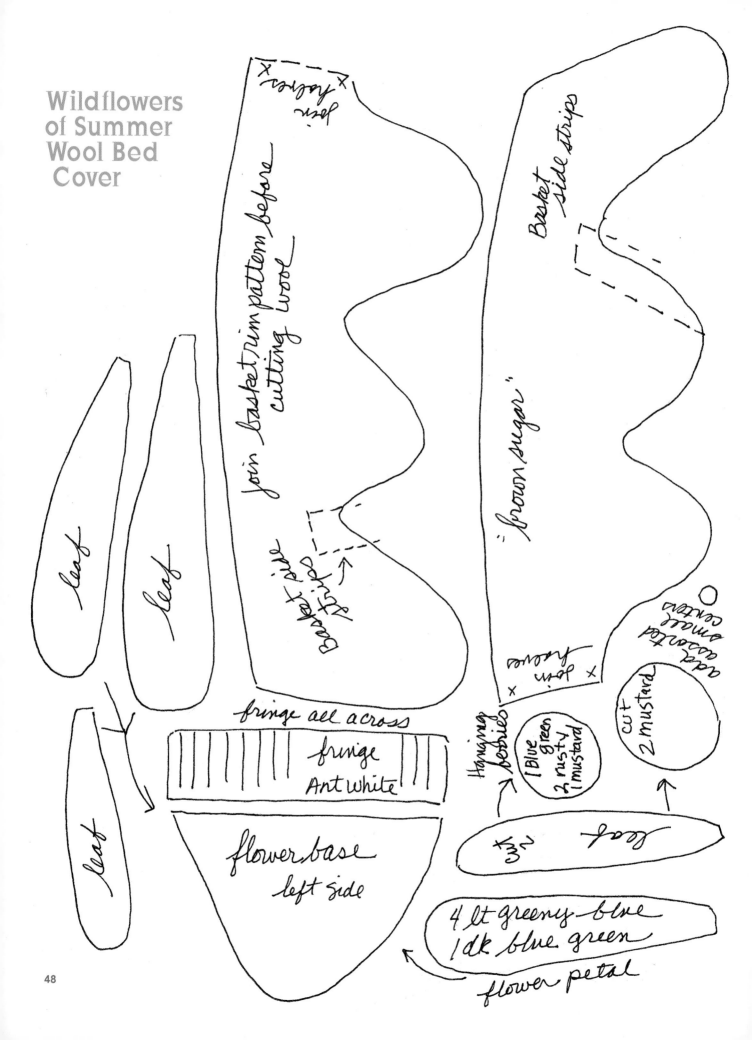

Wildflowers of Summer Wool Bed Cover

leaf

leaf

leaf

leaf

join basket rim pattern before cutting wool

Basket side strips

"brown sugar"

fern holes X

Basket side strips

fern holes X X

Hanging berries

1 blue green 2 rusty 1 mustard

cut 2 mustard

add assorted small center

fringe all across

fringe Ant white

flower base left side

cut 3 2

leaf

4 lt greeny-blue 1 dk blue green

flower petal

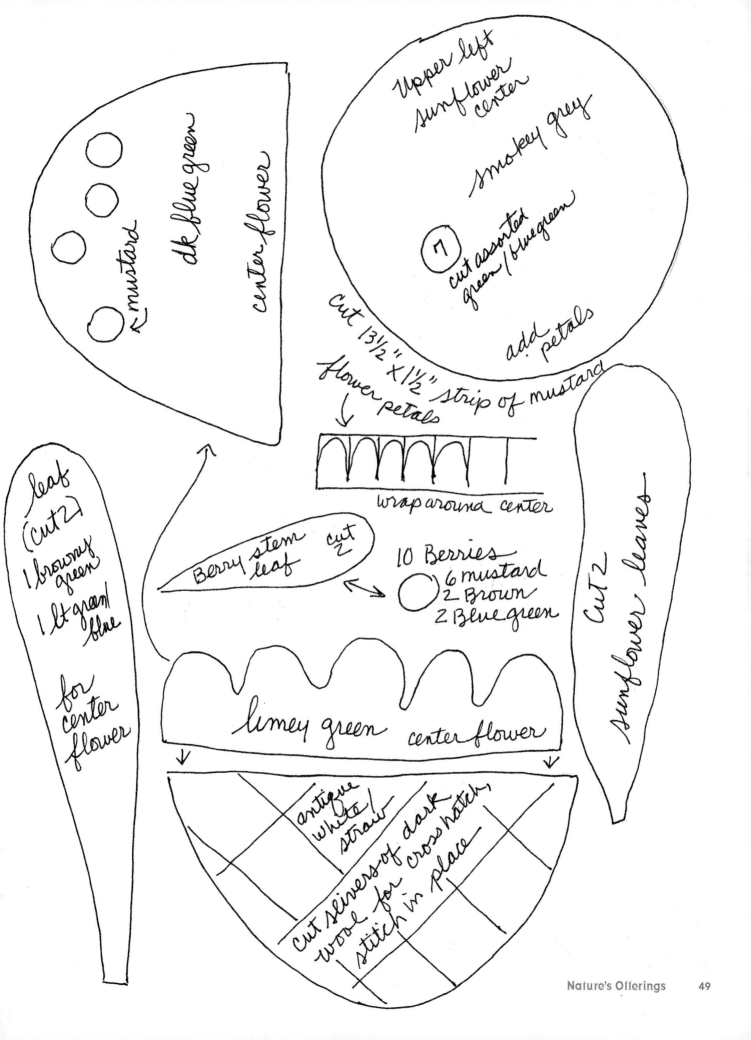

Upper left sunflower center

smokey grey

⑦ cut assorted green / blue green

add petals

dk blue green

center flower

mustard

cut 13½" × 1½" strip of mustard flower petals

wrap around center

leaf (Cut 2)
1 browny green
1 lt green / blue

for center flower

Berry stem leaf   cut 2

10 Berries
6 mustard
2 Brown
2 Blue green

Cut 2 sunflower leaves

limey green   center flower

antique white / straw

cut slivers of dark wool for crosshatch, stitch in place

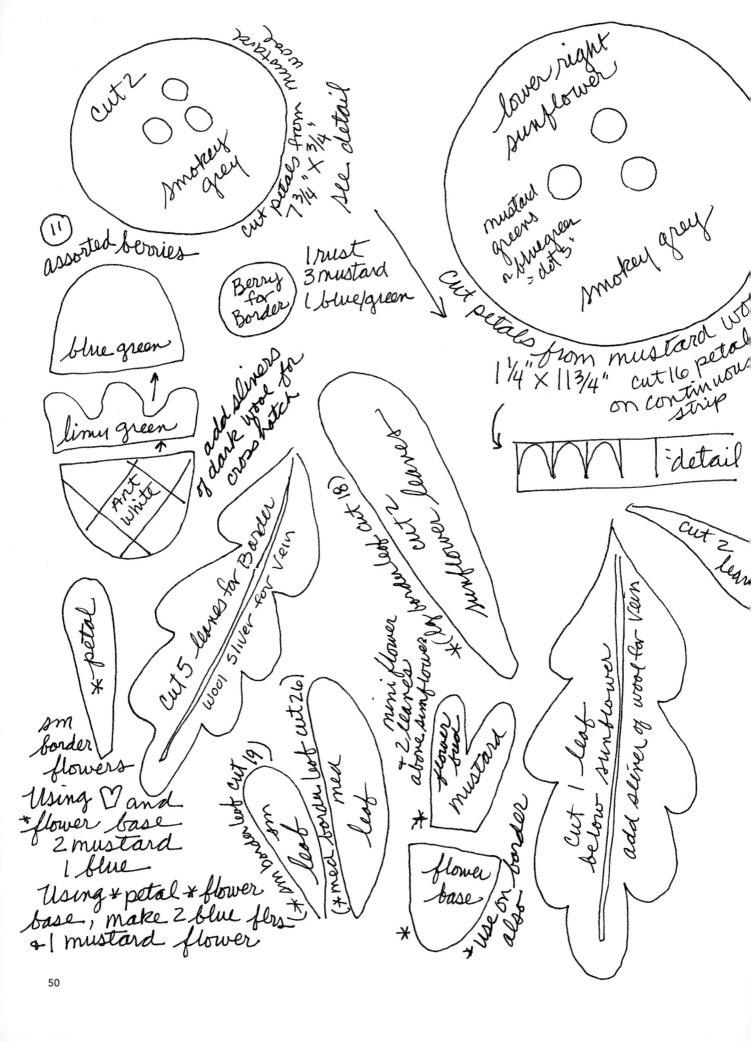

cut 2

smokey grey

Mustard woom

cut petals from
7¼" × ¾"
see detail

11 assorted berries

lower right
sunflower

mustard
greens
& blue/green
= dots.

smokey grey

blue green

Berry
for
Border

1 rust
3 mustard
1 blue/green

cut petals from mustard wool

1¼" × 11¾" cut 16 petals
on continuous
strip

limy green

Ant
white

add slivers
of dark wool for
cross hatch

detail

Cut 5 leaves for Border

wool sliver for vein

mini flower bud & leaf cut 18

sunflower leaves

cut 2
leaf

* petal

sm
border
flowers
Using ♡ and
* flower base
2 mustard
1 blue
Using * petal * flower
base, make 2 blue flrs
+ 1 mustard flower

lg border leaf cut (9)

med border leaf cut (26)

(*) sm border leaf

(*) med border leaf

mini flower
& 2 leaves
above sunflower (*)

* flower
bud
mustard

flower
base

* use on border
also

Cut 1 leaf
below sunflower

add sliver of wool for vein

50

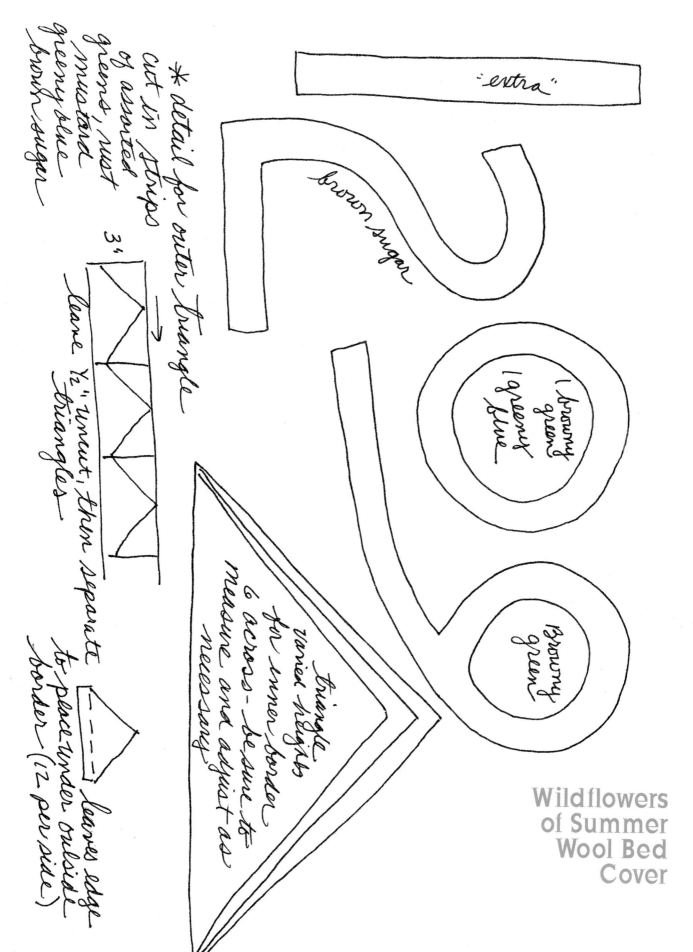

"extra"

brown sugar

1 brown
green
1 green,
blue

brown
green

triangle
varies slightly
for inner border
6 across - be sure to
measure and adjust as
necessary

* detail for outer triangle
cut in strips
of assorted
greens, rust
mustard
green, blue
brown, sugar

3"

leave ½" uncut; then separate
triangles

leaves edge
to place under outside
border (12 per side)

Summer's Bounty

Here are some funny veggies to make. Fill a big old wood dough bowl or a wire basket with them and add any other fruit and veggies you may already have. Of course, I like things to have a purpose (more than just sitting around being cute) so put them to work as pincushions!

Beet

23" end to end

This crazy big veggie can be a beet or turnip. Use it as a folky pincushion or a little fabric sculpture.

Materials needed

20" x 11" plummy colored linen or cotton for beet (see ritdye.com for recipes for colors)

20" x 11" yellow green cotton for leaves

20" x 11" tan cotton calico for leaves

1 1/2" x 2" scrap of brown check cotton for patch

1/2" x 13" Army green wool for leaf veins

20" x 11" fusible webbing for leaf

3 -14" 18-gauge fabric covered floral wires for leaf

Tacky craft glue

Needle, thread

Cotton stuffing

Iron

Assembly

To make the 3 leaves, lay the tan fabric wrong side up, lightly trace with pencil the leaf pattern, alternating leaf top, leaf stem, leaf top to fit on the fabric. Lightly glue a floral wire down the stem center at least 1/2" from leaf top. Layer the fusible web on top, then the green cotton, right side up. Fuse with a hot iron. Once cooled, lay the pattern piece down so the wire will be down the center of the leaf. Either transfer the pattern or just cut out around the pattern piece. Now you have 3 leaves with wire inside. Cut out 3 strips of wool, 1/8" x 13" and lightly glue to tack in place for vein on the green side. I would stitch down the leaf over the vein to include the wire to secure it.

Cut out the beet following the directions on the pattern on page 56. Stitch wrong side out, turn right side out and stuff firmly. Stuff the tip and turn in the raw edge as you go. Leaving little thread ends is good, you will have a more pointy end if you do not try to hide them all. Now gather up the top opening of the beet. Turning in the raw edge, add a bit of glue to the inside. Insert the 3 leaves about 1" in and finish gathering up the top. Make a few stitches to secure the leaves and the gathers. Add a small brown checked patch along the seam if you wish.

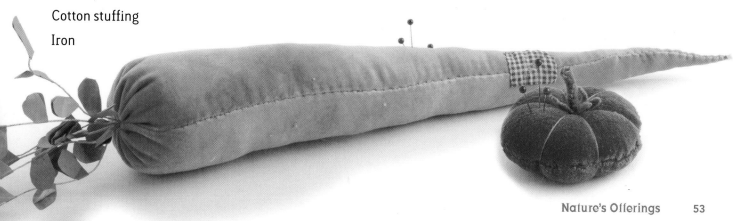

Carrot
22" end to end

This carrot is another veggie to add to your bowl or basket, to use as a pincushion or a folky sculpture. I have used orange velvet, but it would look good in cotton calico or wool. I can never find fake floral stems to use for the leaves so have resorted to making my own, which I think I like much better anyway.

Materials needed

19" x 11" orange velvet for carrot

1" x 2" scrap of brown check cotton for patch

3 green 22-gauge floral wires for leaf stems

6" square light green 'text'-weight paper for paper leaves

Alternative for stem and leaves: white covered floral wire, 6" square white paper, and Rit dye (see ritdye.com to mix color)

Cotton stuffing

Needle and thread

Tacky glue

Assembly

Cut out the carrot (pattern at right). Fold right sides together and stitch from top edge down, leaving the last 3-4" unstitched. Turn right side out and stuff firmly: stuff and stitch down the point of the carrot turning in the raw edges as you go. Leaving a few fabric threads at the end is fine, they looks a bit like little roots. Set this aside.

Make the leaves: cut the floral wires, 3 each 4" and 5 1/2" lengths. Cut out 27 leaves, fold in half, dab some glue on the inside of the fold and place along the wire. On the 5 1/2" stem, use 5 leaves. Begin at the top of the stem and alternate the way they lay (left to right); leave 1" at the bottom of each stem. The 4" stem has 4 leaves glued on in the same manner.

Gather up the top of the carrot, turning in the raw edge as you go. Dab some glue into the top of the carrot and insert the stems. Finish gathering the top closed and secure the stems with a few stitches. Add a small brown checked patch if desired along the seam.

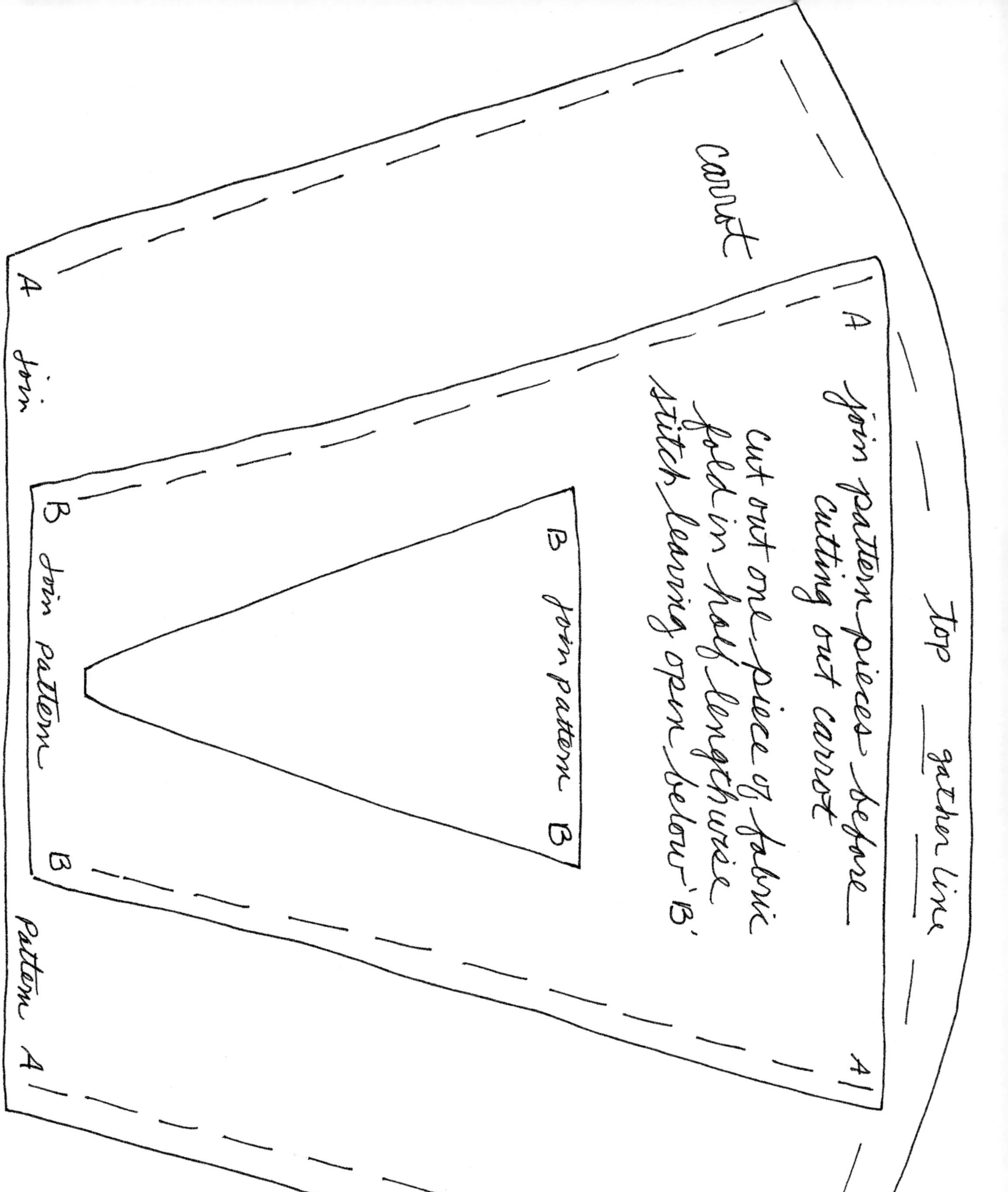

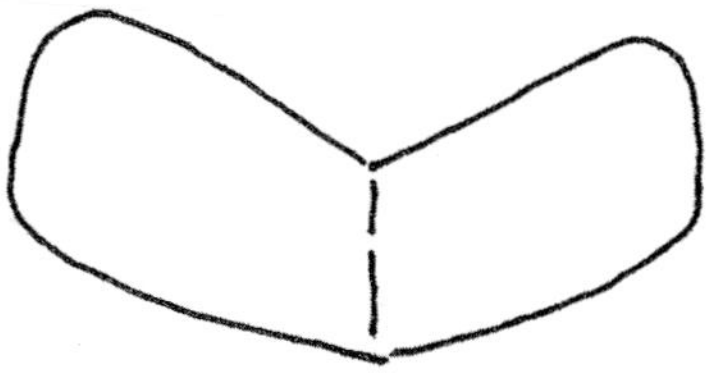

carrot

Top —— gather line

A

join pattern pieces before
cutting out carrot
cut out one piece of fabric
fold in half lengthwise
stitch leaving open below 'B'.

B join pattern B

A join

B join pattern B

B pattern A

cut 27 leaves
from dyed green paper
fold along line in center

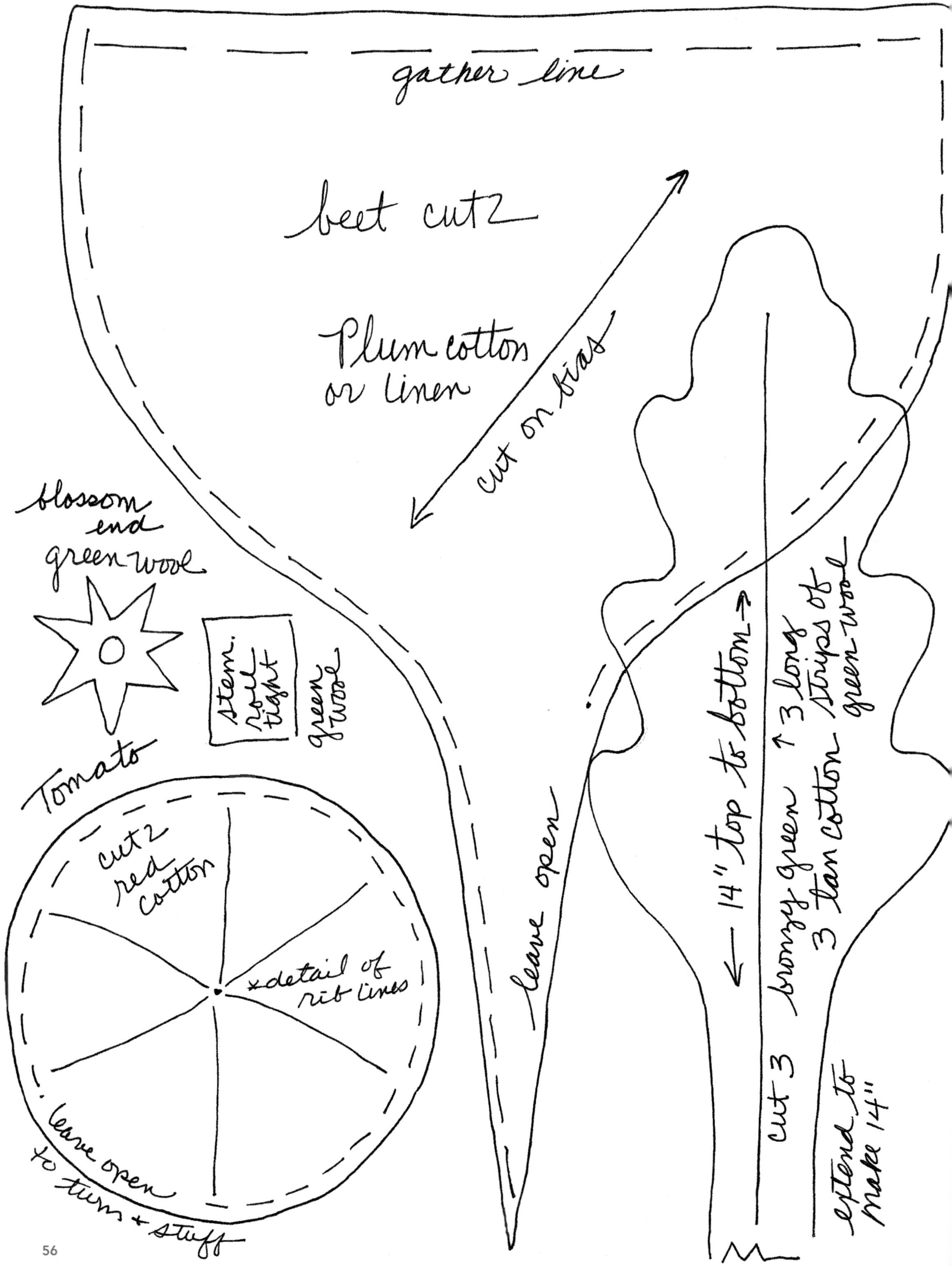

gather line

beet cut2

Plum cotton
or linen

cut on bias

blossom
end
green wool

Stem.
roll
tight

green wool

Tomato

cut 2
red
cotton

detail of
rib lines

leave open
to turn + stuff

leave open

14" top to bottom →

cut 3   bronzy green   ↑ 3 long strips of
3 tan cotton   green wool

extend to
make 14"

56

Tomato
3" diameter

This is not so big; it's a traditional pincushion shape. I've seen them forever in varied colors and usually with a strawberry emery attached. For fun make multiples and fill a bowl or glass apothecary jar. You can easily create these in different fabrics and sizes. I used red cotton velvet but if you cannot find any red velvet, go to Ritdye.com to get the recipe to dye a light velvet. You could also make this in cotton, wool or calico fabric.

Materials needed

4" x 8" red cotton velvet for tomato

2" square green wool for stem and blossom end

1 yard green embroidery floss (6 strands ribs on tomato)

Cotton stuffing

Needle and thread

Assembly

Cut out the tomato (see pattern at left). Stitch right sides together, leave opening to turn right side out. Stuff (not too firmly), stitch closed. Using the embroidery floss with a knot at the end, bring your needle up through the bottom center of the tomato. Pull the knot to the inside, then bring the thread around the side and back up through the center. Repeat 5 more times, evenly spacing as you go and pulling just enough that the thread indents a bit to define the tomato shape. Knot on the top center of the tomato.

Cut out stem and blossom end. Roll the stem tightly, stitch securely, and tack this in the center top. Slip the blossom end down over the stem and tack in place. Now you have a pincushion to put among your sewing necessities - or another veggie to display.

Summer Fruit Basket

17" x 14"

There is nothing quite like it, when summer arrives and there is wonderful fresh fruit. This design was inspired by an old fruit basket Theorem painting an Early American traditional art form of painting on velvet, paper or other materials using layers of stencils. This is frameable or would make a great pillow front.

Materials needed

18" x 15" tiny brown check cotton homespun for background

18" x 15" flannel or thin batting for stabilizing the background

9" x 3" light brown wool for basket and stems

3" x 5" dark brown wool for basket and seeds

3" x 10" light red cotton for watermelon

12" x 1/2" green wool for melon rind

12" x 1/2" white wool for melon rind

3" x 7" assorted medium green wools for leaves

3" x 5" assorted dark green wools for leaves

5" x 7" green polka dot cotton for pear

2" x 3" light orange wool for cherries

2" x 3" dark red wool for strawberry

4" x 5" pumpkin velvet or wool for pumpkin

10" x 2" purple wool and 1 1/2" x 3" purple cotton or linen for grapes

Tan thread (or color of your choice)

Hand sewing supplies

Assembly

Cut out the pattern pieces (see pages 60-61) and use the photo as a guide. Cut a 1/2" x 8" light brown wool strip, center this 3" above the bottom edge of the background fabric. Position the watermelon 1 3/4" above this strip: tilt it slightly to the left, adding the rind as instructed on the pattern. Position the pear over the melon, then add the pumpkin - these both will rest on basket base. Stitch in place, turn under raw edges where necessary. Add the stems and leaves to these, then stitch the rib detail onto the pumpkin.

Basket: cut 9 - 3" x 1/2" dark brown wool ribs. Place over fruit, angling out the outside ribs. Cut a light brown strip of wool 1/4" x 9", weave over and under the upright ribs, stitch basket in place.

Cherries: cut light brown stems, 1/4" x 5 1/2". Cut this in half lengthwise to make thin stems, leave 1 stem longer than the other. Add orange cherries and a small snip of dark brown wool as the blossom end of the cherries. Add 2 leaves, stitch in place.

Strawberry: stitch down with cap and stem so it overlaps edge of basket.

Melon seeds: add these from dark brown wool.

To finish, frame with your choice of frames or make a pillow with velvet back and stuff.

Summer Fruit Basket

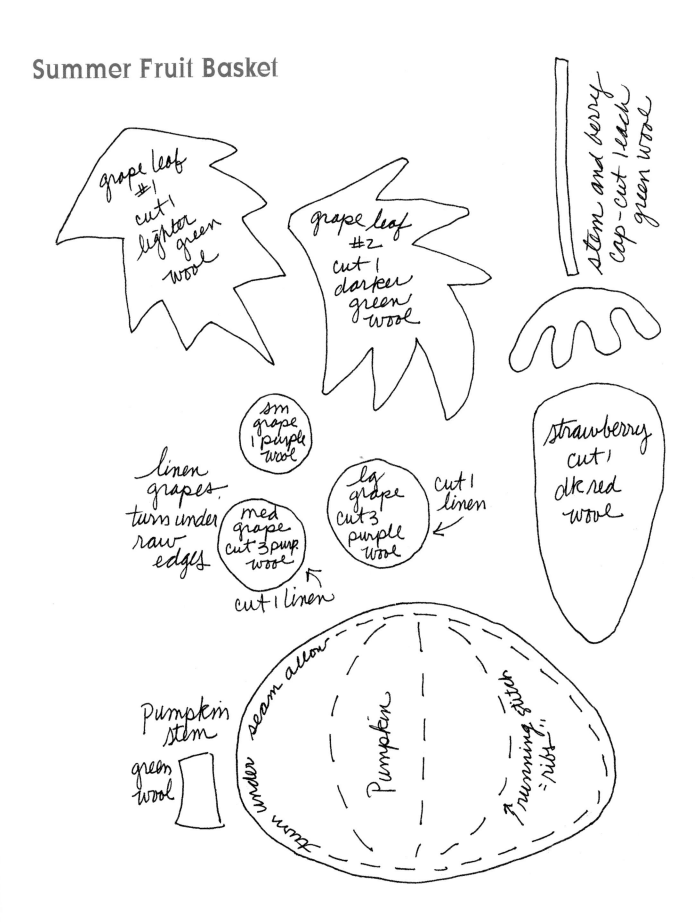

grape leaf #1 cut 1 lighter green wool

grape leaf #2 cut 1 darker green wool

stem and berry cap – cut 1 each green wool

sm grape 1 purple wool

linen grapes, turn under raw edges

med grape cut 3 purp. wool

lg grape cut 3 purple wool

cut 1 linen

cut 1 linen

strawberry cut 1 dk red wool

Pumpkin stem green wool

turn under seam allow

Pumpkin

running stitch = "ribs"

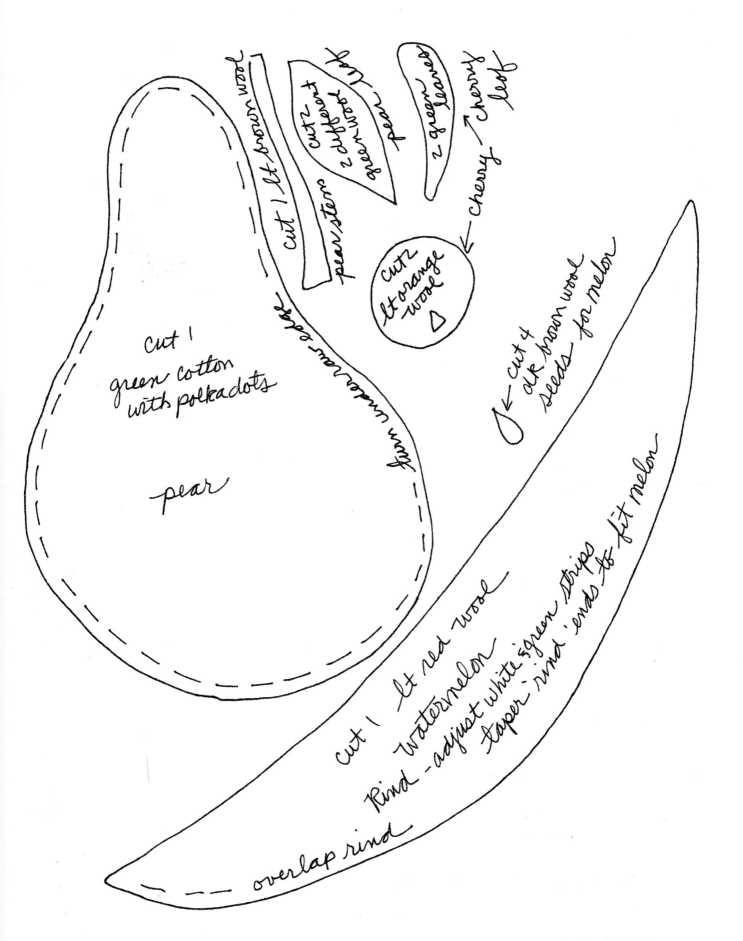

cut 1 lt brown wool

cut 1 lt brown wool
pear stem

cut 2 different
2 greens
pear leaf

2 greens
cherry leaf

cherry

cut 2
lt orange
wool

cut 4
dk brown wool
seeds for melon

cut 1
green cotton
with polka dots

funnel under leaf

pear

cut 1 lt red wool
watermelon
Rind - adjust white & green strips
taper rind ends to fit melon

overlap rind

"The poetry of the earth is never dead"
– John Keats

Bee Skep in the Garden
6 1/4" x 6 3/4"

I have always liked the quote above by Keats – it makes me think of gardens I have had. There is poetry sitting in a garden on a warm summer day with a slight breeze blowing. The flowers move gently and smell wonderful and there is the hum and buzz of insects and bees hard at work. I used to have some beautiful foxgloves growing in the garden and it was so funny to see the big old bumble bees enter the bell shaped flowers, barely fitting inside. The bee would buzz and the whole flower would move, then the bee would back out full of pollen and enter the next flower. I have had years where nothing but queen Ann's Lace grew and another when it was all Black-eyed Susans. I love a garden, it is so relaxed and unhurried.

This garden paper cut was made to remind me of my gardens. I used old journal paper I found but you could use plain paper lightly stained with tea or coffee. Of course, there are wonderful papers in hobby shops and scrapbooking stores.

You need a good sharp pencil to transfer the design: you cut this design folded and must have the fold in the right place. Tiny sharp scissors are a must, cuticle scissors work great. Cut out the inside areas first then the outside, when you finish open it up and like magic, you have a bee skep in the garden. Pick a background paper color of your choice and frame it so the glass will help protect the finished piece. I used a glue stick to mount it to the background. Write the quote, by John Keats using a white ink pen found in scrapbooking stores.

Materials needed

8 1/2" x 11" journal paper
Sharp small scissors such as cuticle scissors
Glue stick
Sharp pencil
White ink pen
Colored paper for backing
Frame of your choice

"The poetry of the earth
is never dead."
— John Keats

cut on folded paper

paper cut pattern

1870 Urn Table Runner
16" x 40"

The colors on this mat are great for fall - an old urn filled with branches of flowers and berries with a little bird perched on one to sample some of those berries. When I originally made this, I could not find dark linen so I dyed my linen with a bit of black dye for a dark charcoal look. There are dark linens or cottons available at quilt shops but you could even use a piece of wool for the background.

Materials needed

17" x 41" linen for background (optional: 16" x 40" wool)
17" x 41" cotton backing
8" x 8" golden brown plaid for urn
4" x 5" antique white wool for flowers and seeds
12" x 3" soft yellow gold wool for flower petals
3" x 3" tweed wool for bird
4" x 6" brown/black herringbone wool for flower centers and bases
8" x 5" rust wool for pomegranates, bird wing, and berries
3" x 5" pumpkin wool for hanging berries
3" x 8" dark brown wool for numbers
9" x 11" Army green wool for leaves
40" x 14" Army green wool for stems, tendrils, wool edging
3" x 5" dark brown wool for the 1870 numbers
Scrap of tan wool for bird beak and berries

Maggie also used the 1870 Urn pattern for this hooked rug.

Assembly

If using linen or cotton turn under 1/2" all around. Refer to the photo as a guide for placing pieces to appliqué. First tear 3 strips of Army green wool 3" x 40" and set aside for edging. Cut strips for stems 1/4" x 18": cut several and cut some about 1/8" wide as well. The urn should be placed just above the center of the bottom edge of the mat. Lay out the 2 longest stems, each 18" long. Using them and the space available, lay out the rest of the design. Appliqué all in place using a simple whip stitch. The edging is something I use a lot: measure

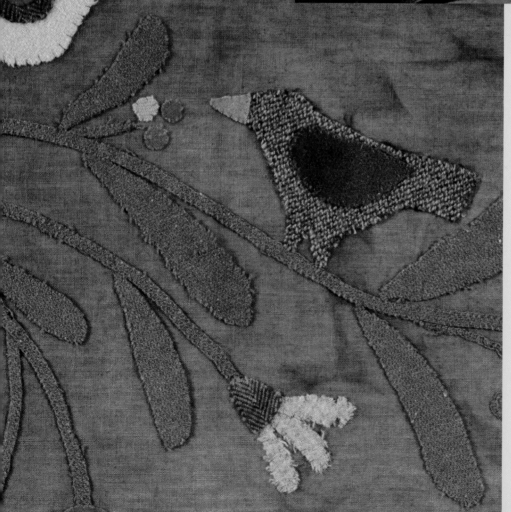

2 of the Army green wool strips that were set aside to be sure they are the same length as the runner and cut the remaining one into 2 - 16" lengths for the sides. Cut the 40" strips into 16 sections, leaving 1 edge uncut (see diagram), then cut each section into a point. Cut the shorter pieces in 6 sections, then cut them into points. Pin the uncut edge under the sides and length of the runner, stitch in place. Cover the back of the table runner with cotton backing, turning under raw edges. Stitch in place.

Urn
golden brown plaid

1870

Numbers:
dark brown
or black wool

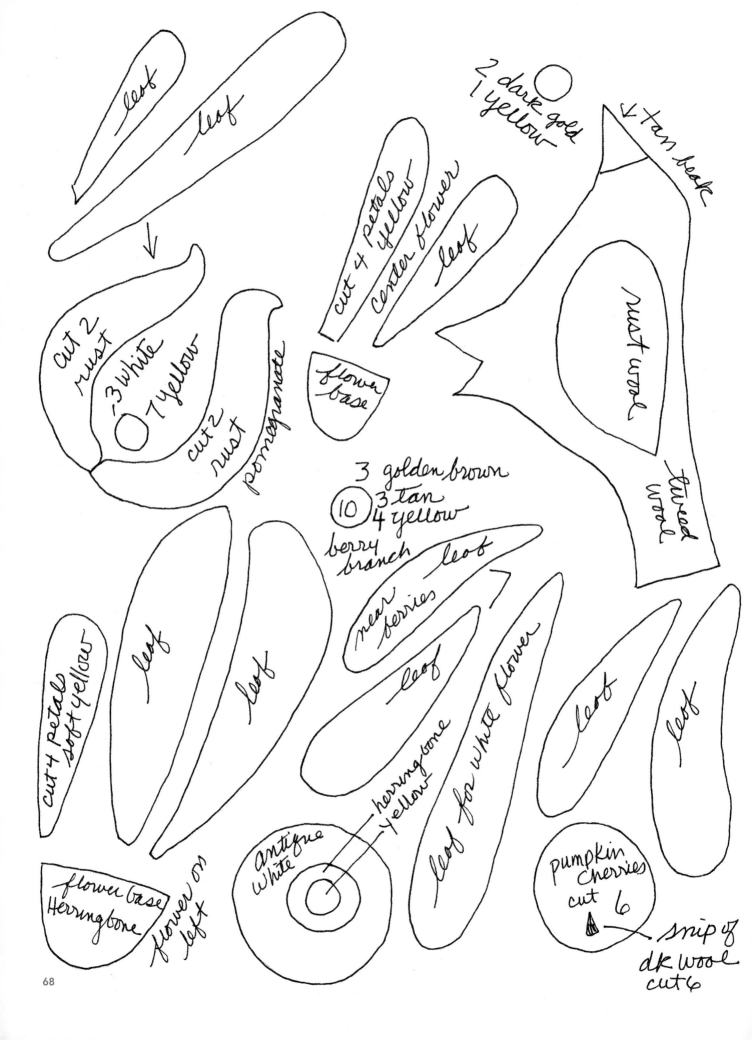

leaf

leaf

2 dark gold
1 yellow

↘ tan beak

cut 4 Petals
yellow

Center flower

leaf

Cut 2
rust

~3 white
1 yellow

cut 2
rust

pomegranate

rust wool

flower
base

Tweed
wool

3 golden brown
10 3 tan
4 yellow

berry
branch

near
berries

leaf

leaf

leaf

cut 4 petals
soft yellow

leaf

leaf

leaf

leaf

herringbone
yellow

leaf for white flower

leaf

flower base
Herringbone

flower on left

Antique
White

pumpkin
Cherries
cut 6

snip of
dk wool
cut 6

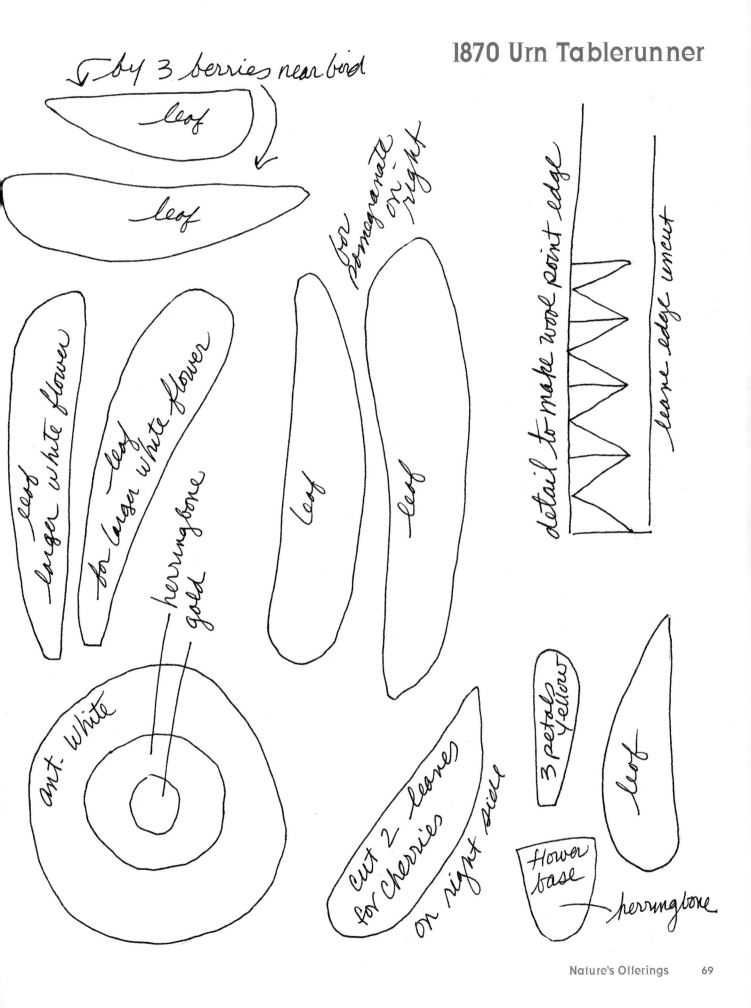

by 3 berries near bird

leaf

leaf

leaf

for larger white flower

leaf for larger white flower

herringbone gold

for pomegranate on right

leaf

leaf

detail to make wool point edge

leave edge uncut

ant. white

cut 2 leaves for cherries on right piece

3 petals yellow

flower base

leaf

herringbone

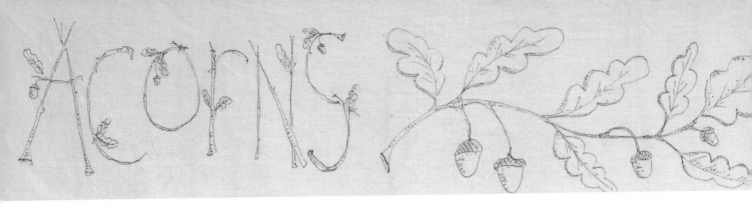

Acorn and Leaf Needlekeep Pincushion

9" x 3"

This is a sweet little needlekeep that reminds me of a souvenir that might be found at one of those shops up in the mountains.

Materials needed

6" x 12" brown wool for leaf

3" x 5" brown check flannel for needles

Scrap of muslin for label

5" x 2" tan wool or cotton for acorn nut

5" x 2" dark brown wool for acorn cap and stem

Golden green 6-ply embroidery floss to attach leaf and acorn

Large-eyed needle for floss

Cotton stuffing

Permanent black ink pen for label

3/4" button

Assembly

Cut out 4 brown leaves using the leaf pattern on page 72. Sew 2 pairs of leaves together so you have 2 thick leaves. Cut out the flannel patch, center it on 1 set of leaves and stitch in place, turning under the raw edge. Cut out muslin for the 'needles' label, write the word "Needles" using the pen. Stitch in the center of the other set of leaves. Be sure when you stack the leaves they match up. Sew the 2 leaves together, securing the button on top of the leaf with the label.

Using the acorn pattern on page 72, follow the directions (on page 76) to make the larger acorn. Cut 3 – 12" strands of the embroidery floss. Stitch through the top of the acorn cap, pull floss to even the ends and braid or twist for 1 3/4". Tie a knot around the button to secure the acorn, continue braiding or twisting floss another 2 1/2", tie a knot, leave the ends as a tassel. You now have a little needlekeep with an acorn pincushion.

cut 4
Brown wool

flannel
cut 1

acorn
cap

Needles

tan
cotton
cut 2

stems
roll
tight

to make
acorn use
diagram in
"Every leaf..."

paper
leaf

Every leaf
speaks
bliss
to me
falling
from
the
Autumn
tree.
Bronte

When I was little my family would go on vacation and spend time camping at some of the National Parks. I loved the quiet and the smell of the forest, I can still smell the pine trees. Now my parents' idea of camping was a cute little 16' Airstream trailer, complete with a kitchen and a tiny bathroom! I remember the time my sister and I spent at picnic tables, making stuff to keep us busy. There were always plenty of twigs, leaves and acorns and pinecones to make something out of. I have grouped these projects together because they remind me of that time and they are quick and easy. I can still imagine sitting out there on a warm fall day at on old picnic table under some big old pine trees having a grand time...it doesn't really take much to make me happy!

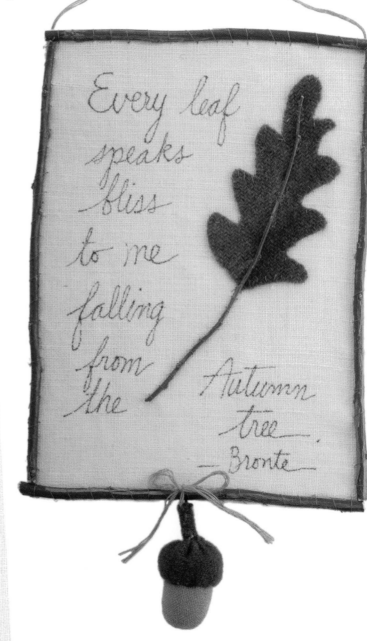

Camp Leaf Picture
5" x 7"

This is a simple and quick project complete with a self frame but could be adapted and put in a purchased frame without the twigs.

Materials needed

5" x 7" cardboard (from cereal box or cracker box)
5" x 7" cotton flannel
6" x 8" linen or muslin
5" x 7" brown wool for backing
4" square brown wool for leaf, acorn cap and stem
2" x 3" green gold wool for acorn
Green gold 6-ply embroidery floss to tie acorn, hanger
5 1/2" - 6" thin twig or brown wool scrap for stem on leaf
24" of 1/4" twig for frame
Cotton stuffing or cotton balls to stuff acorn
Glue stick
Tacky glue
Permanent black ink pen
Needle and thread for hand sewing

Assembly

Cover your cardboard with the flannel using the glue stick - do this on the non-printed side of the cardboard. Set aside. Cut out the leaf and stitch it to

(continued on page 76)

Camp Projects

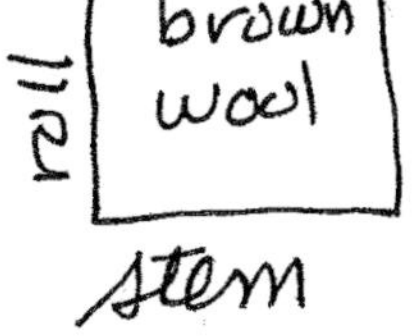

Every leaf
speaks
Bliss
to me
falling
from
the
Autumn
tree

— Bronte

TWIG

TWIG

TWIG

TWIG

cut 1 brown wool

leaf

Twig or wool strip

cut 2
Acorn
green
gold

roll

brown
wool

stem

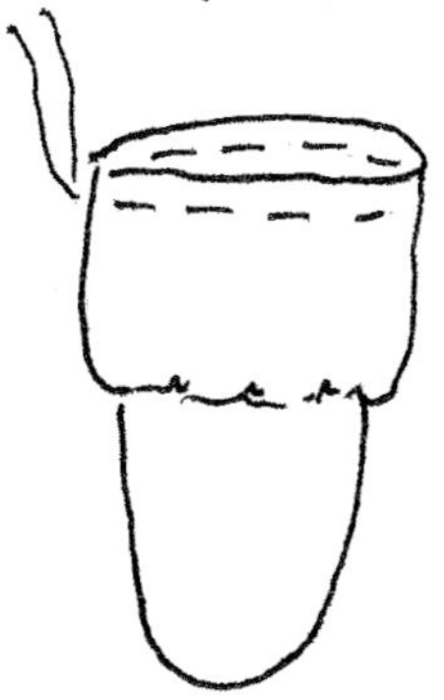

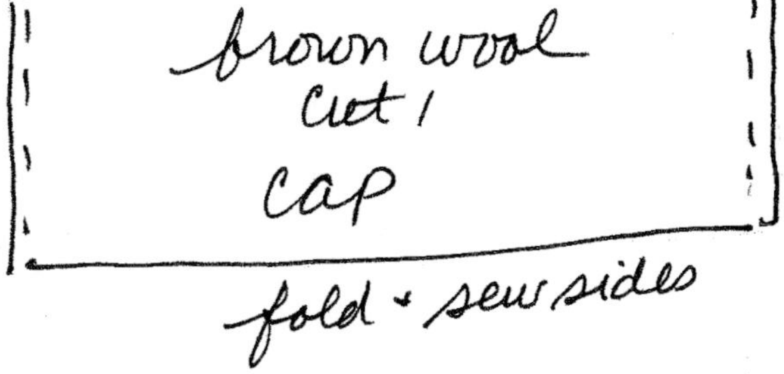

tie Acorn
here

brown wool
cut 1
cap

fold + sew sides

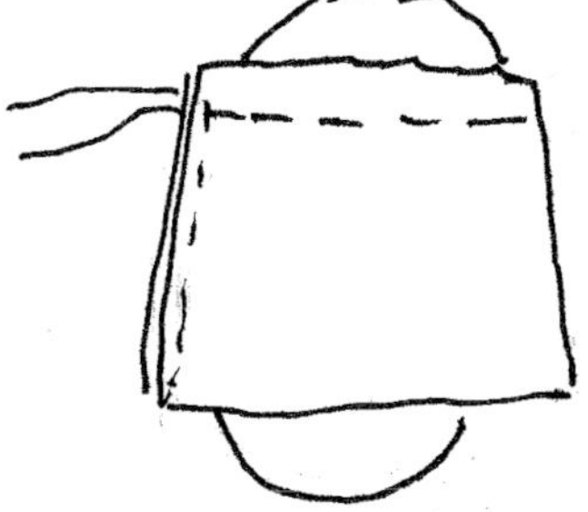

the linen using the provided picture for placement. Add the twig, daubing the glue stick to the twig to help hold it in place. Stitch over the twig to secure it. Using the pen, write the verse onto the linen (be sure to test the pen on a scrap of the same material to make sure it does not bleed). Once completed, lay the linen face down and lay the flannel side of the cardboard on top. Use the glue stick to adhere the "seam allowance" to the back side of the cardboard. Set the piece of wool on top and stitch all around.

Twig Frame

Cut the twigs to fit the outside edges of the finished piece, measuring the top and bottom edges first, then the sides. Use a tiny bit of tacky glue to hold the twig in place, doing only one side at a time, then use a needle and thread stitch over the twig into the background down the length to secure it in place. Repeat for the other 3 sides.

Hanging Acorn

Use the acorn pattern on page 75 and cut 2 pieces of green gold wool. Stitch a narrow seam around the curved edge, leaving the top open. Turn right side out and stuff firmly. Baste stitch and gather the top opening. Cut 1 brown wool cap, Stitch together the narrow edge. Place cap over the nut, wrong side out. Ease/gather the edge one-quarter of the way below the top of the nut, stitch and secure. Pull the cap up; stuff and gather the top edge closed, tucking in the raw edge. Roll the stem piece tightly and secure with a couple of stitches. Stitch the stem to the acorn. Using 8" of the 6-ply embroidery floss, catch the top of the acorn stem and bring the floss up between the linen and the twig in the center of the bottom - tie a small bow to hold the acorn in place. Use 10" of the floss for a hanger, attaching at the 2 top corners. Now you have a little camp souvenir.

Nature Notebook, Leaf Journal, and Acorn Ornament

Another camp project to make. You will have a little notebook and a journal to jot down things you observe while in the great outdoors or just keep anything you might want to remember. I actually used real leaves for my pattern, I believe both were oak leaves. The little acorn ornament has paper leaves and can be hung on a knob or your Christmas tree.

These two little books are constructed very similarly using bits of cotton, linen, brown paper, twigs and a small piece of floral wire.

Nature Notebook

This leaf-shaped notebook with its twig label will display perfectly with all your nature finds.

Materials needed

4 1/2" x 16" green over-dyed linen or cotton
(see ritdye.com)

4 1/2" x 16" fusible webbing

4 1/2" x 16" brown kraft paper (you may want to dip paper in dye or tea to discolor randomly)

Additional brown paper for pages (lunch sacks are perfect)

Thin twigs

Tan dye or tea or walnut ink spray

Large-eyed needle

12" length of tan string

Glue stick

Iron

Assembly

To construct the leaves, it is best to layer the linen (wrong side up), fusible web, and brown paper. Press with a hot iron to fuse together. Cut out 2 large leaves - be sure to flip the pattern so they fit together. Following the diagram on page 79, cut the thin twigs to spell out the word 'Nature' on the leaf top. I used the glue stick to hold the twigs in place, then stitched over them to secure them. Do this by stitching through the leaf and over the twig back into the leaf – the stitches do not have to be close together. Cut out about 10 leaves using notebook paper pattern. Stack the pages between the covers and use the large needle and string to tie it all together, ending with a bow or knot on top.

Assembly

This Leaf Journal is constructed similar to the Nature Notebook. The difference is the floral wire needs to be cut to fit 1 leaf from tip to stem end. This is lightly glued to paper before the fusible web goes on, then add muslin and fuse with a hot iron. Cut out the pages from brown paper or brown lunch sacks using the inner pattern on the leaf - hold it all together by stitching through all layers at one end with the string and the needle. Tie a bow to finish. I used a black permanent ink pen to lightly mark the veins of the leaf and write 'nature notes" on the first page. Both of these leafy notebooks look great along with any other of nature's offerings.

Leaf Journal

This small journal has a wired cover so you can bend it open as desired.

Materials needed

5" x 8" muslin dyed golden green
(see ritdye.com)
5" x 8" fusible webbing
Brown kraft paper or brown lunch sacks
One fabric covered floral wire
Large-eyed needle
8" length of tan string
Permanent black ink pen

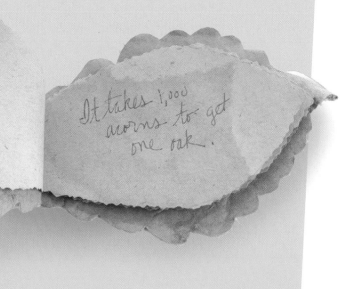

Acorn Ornament

This large single acorn is the same used as part of the Acorn and Leaf Needlekeep (see page 70) but this time it has paper leaves. This acorn can be made in multiples in different wools and cottons, even velvets. A single acorn could hang from a cupboard knob.

Materials needed

5" x 2"dark brown wool for cap and stem
5" x 2" black cotton for nut
Cotton stuffing or cotton balls
12" length of golden green 6-ply embroidery floss
Scrap of old book page or journal paper for leaves

Assembly

Follow the instructions on page 76 to make the acorn. Stitch through the top of the acorn cap with the length of floss. Knot, then bring the ends up even and tie off to make a loop for hanging.

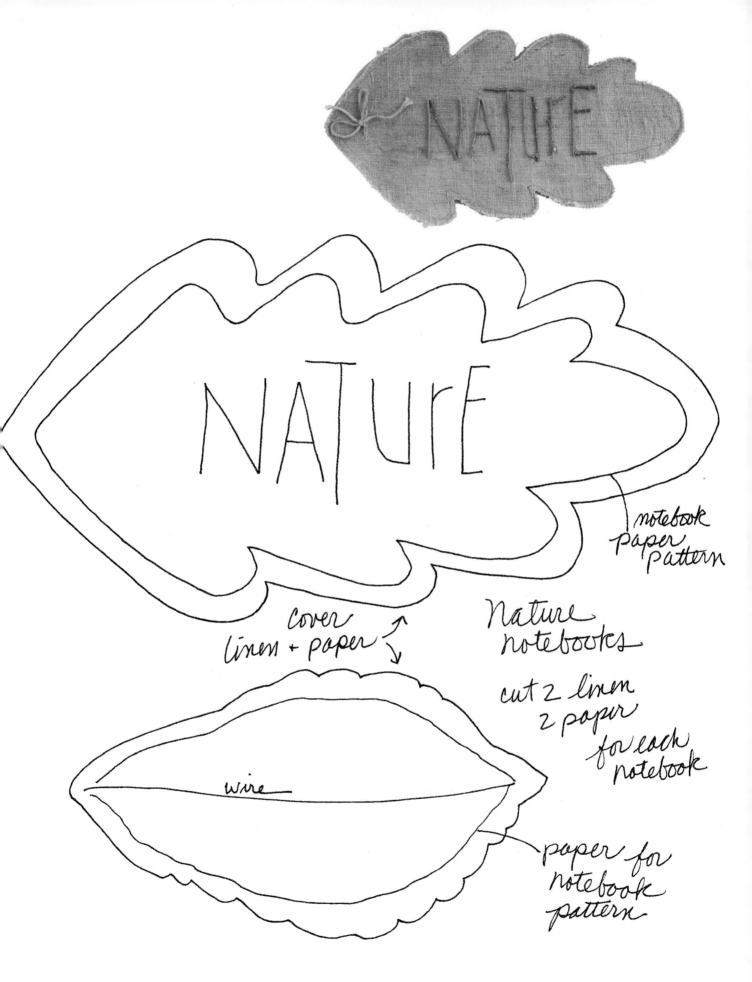

NATURE

notebook
paper
pattern

Nature
notebooks

cut 2 linen
2 paper
for each
notebook

cover
linen + paper

wire

paper for
notebook
pattern

Autumn Pears

The pear has a pleasing shape and had been reproduced in art it seems forever. I have collected stone, wax, and fabric pears in many different sizes and materials. I've created three projects here for you, a Large Green Pear, a Sewing Make-do Pear and a small Pear Ornament.

Large Green Pear

Materials needed

13" x 28" mustard green cotton muslin for pear
(optional: use natural muslin and dye according to color chart at ritdye.com)

5" x 2" brown wool for stem and blossom end

1 1/2" x 2 1/2" scrap of brown check cotton for patch

Cotton stuffing

6" floral wire

Birdcage grit (used as weight): about a cupful

Small sandwich-size plastic bag to hold grit

Tape to secure plastic bag

Tacky glue

Needle and thread

Assembly

Cut out 2 pear shapes (use the patterns on page 84) on the bias from the green muslin. Stitch a 1/4" seam around the pear, right sides together, leaving bottom open. Turn right side out and stuff firmly with cotton stuffing until about 3/4 full. Put the bird grit in plastic bag and secure the bag with tape. Put the plastic bag with the birdcage grit in the pear and continue stuffing, smoothing the stuffing around the bag as needed. Use double thread to baste stitch around the bottom then gather, turning in the raw edge as you draw it closed, stuffing firmly as necessary. *Hint:* as you gather, continue to stitch around again in the same way as before, this will help to close the bottom and help to not break your thread. Cut the stem and blossom end from brown wool, tack the blossom end over the gathered bottom. Fold the 6" floral wire in half and lay it along the long edge of stem wool and roll tightly, stitching edge firmly in place. To attach the stem, snip a small hole at the top of the pear but NOT in the seam. Dab a bit of glue in the opening, insert the stem and tack it in place. Add the brown checked patch if desired.

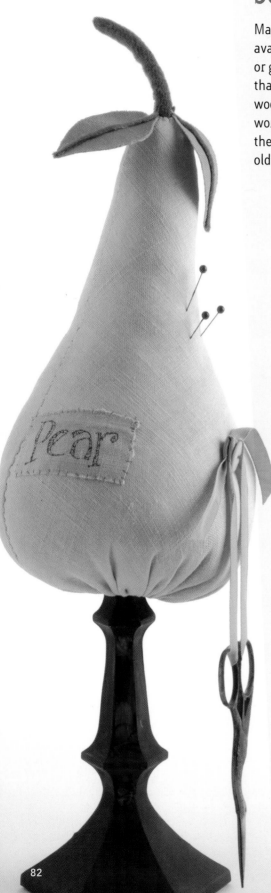

Sewing Make-do Pear

Make-do is a name given to objects that were created making "do" with what is available, old pincushions were sometimes found on top of a broken candlestick or goblet, things that could no longer be used . Many other things were given that name, maybe a wooden handle replacing a broken china one, I have seen wooden bowls that were cracked wired together. We live in a very disposable world but in previous centuries you needed to repair or make an object do since there may not be any replacement available. You can see this process often in old quilts where tiny bits of fabric are stitched together to get one more square.

Materials needed

13" x 28" off-white linen for pear

1" x 3 1/4" brown wool for stem

Linen scrap for "pear" label

3" square each: green cotton, tan calico and fusible web for leaves

Scrap of green wool leaf vein

9" floral wire for stem (6" for stem, 2 – 1 1/2" pieces wire for leaves)

1/2" button to hang scissors

16" - 1/2" pale green ribbon to hang scissors

Cotton stuffing

Permanent ink pen

Tacky glue

8" glass candlestick

Dark brown acrylic paint and brush

Needle and thread

Assembly

Paint the glass candlestick with dark brown paint and set aside. Using the large pear pattern on page 84, cut out and sew pear. When you gather up the bottom, insert the top part of the candlestick with some glue on the end, gather tightly around the candlestick. To make the stem: fold the floral wire in half, lay it along the long edge of brown wool and roll tightly, stitching the edge firmly in place. To attach the stem, snip a small hole in the top of the pear but NOT in the seam, dab a bit of glue in the opening, insert the stem and tack it in place with a few stitches. The leaves are made by laying brown calico wrong side up: lightly mark the large leaf pattern for 2 leaves. Tack 1 1/2" floral wire lightly with glue down the center of each leaf, lay the fusible web on top, then green cotton right side up. Fuse with a hot iron. Mark again, feeling for the wire and using it as a guide to center leaf pattern. Cut out the leaves, add sliver of wool for vein. Stitch down and tack the leaves at the stem base. Use a permanent pen to write the word "pear" on a linen scrap patch, stitch to pear. Sew a button onto the pear. Loop a ribbon through the scissor handles, tie a knot in the ends and hang on the button.

Pear Ornament

This pear has paper leaves cut from an old damaged book or journal paper - you could also use paper from a scrapbooking store. It can be made to hang from an old cupboard knob or make up multiples in varied color and fill a wood bowl or ironstone compote just for fun.

Materials needed

8 1/2" x 11" soft green cotton muslin (same as for Large Green Pear) for pear

2 1/2" x 3" old book or journal paper for leaves

Cotton stuffing

2" twig for stem

12" length of brown 6-ply embroidery floss to hang pear

Dab of brown paint for blossom end

Tacky glue

Assembly

Cut out 2 pear pieces on the bias. Stitch right sides together leaving the bottom open. Turn right side out and stuff firmly. Gather along the bottom, stuffing as necessary but leave the raw edges out, forming the blossom end. Secure thread, dab raw edge with brown paint. Snip a small hole at the top of the pear but not in the seam. Dab some glue to the end of the twig and insert it into the hole. Stitch it closed securely. Add floss at top to form hanger. Cut out paper leaves, glue to the base of stem

Patterns on pages 84-85.

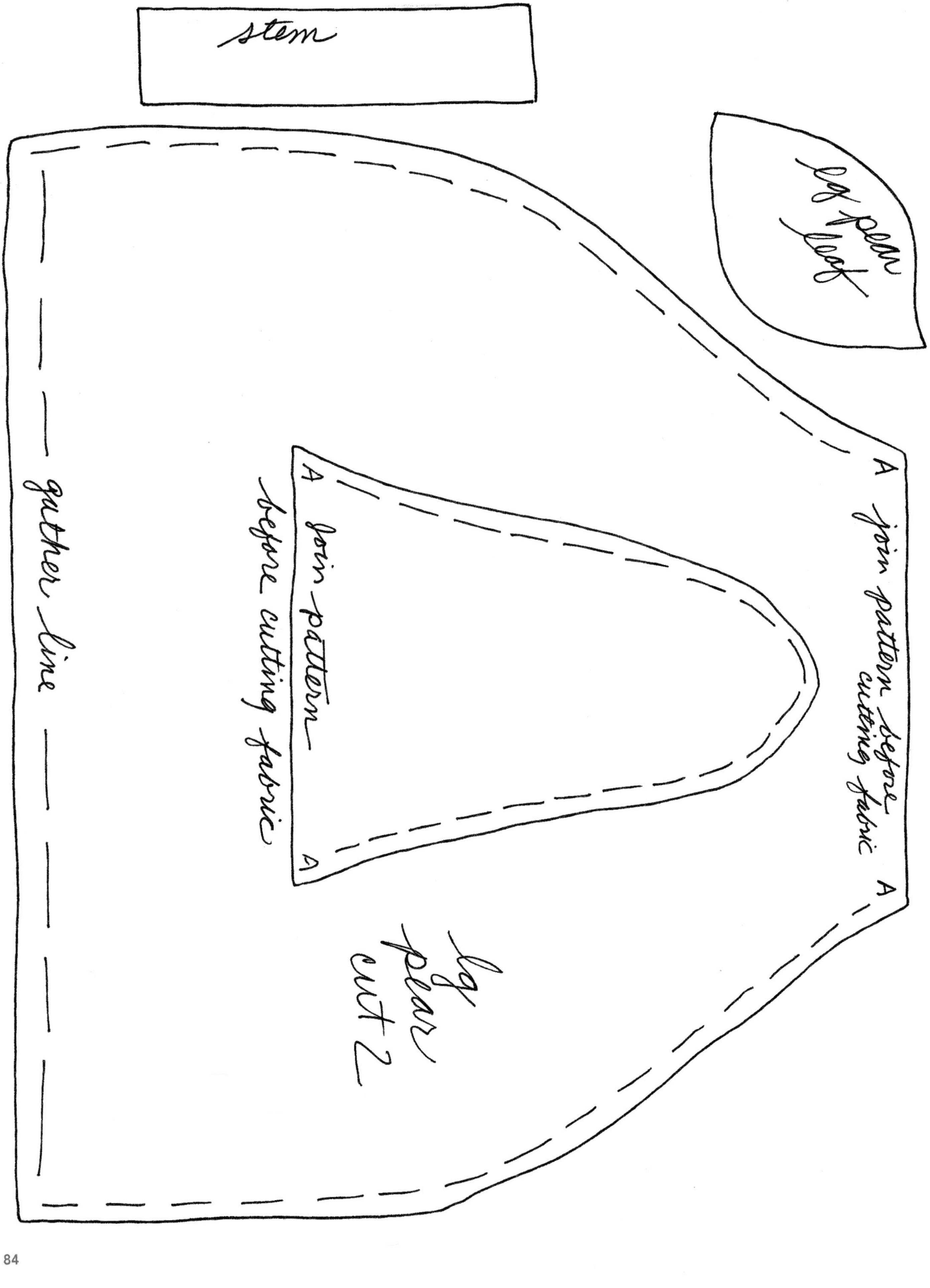

stem

lg pear leaf

join pattern before cutting fabric

join pattern before cutting fabric

A

A

A

A

A

A

lg pear cut 2

gather line

84

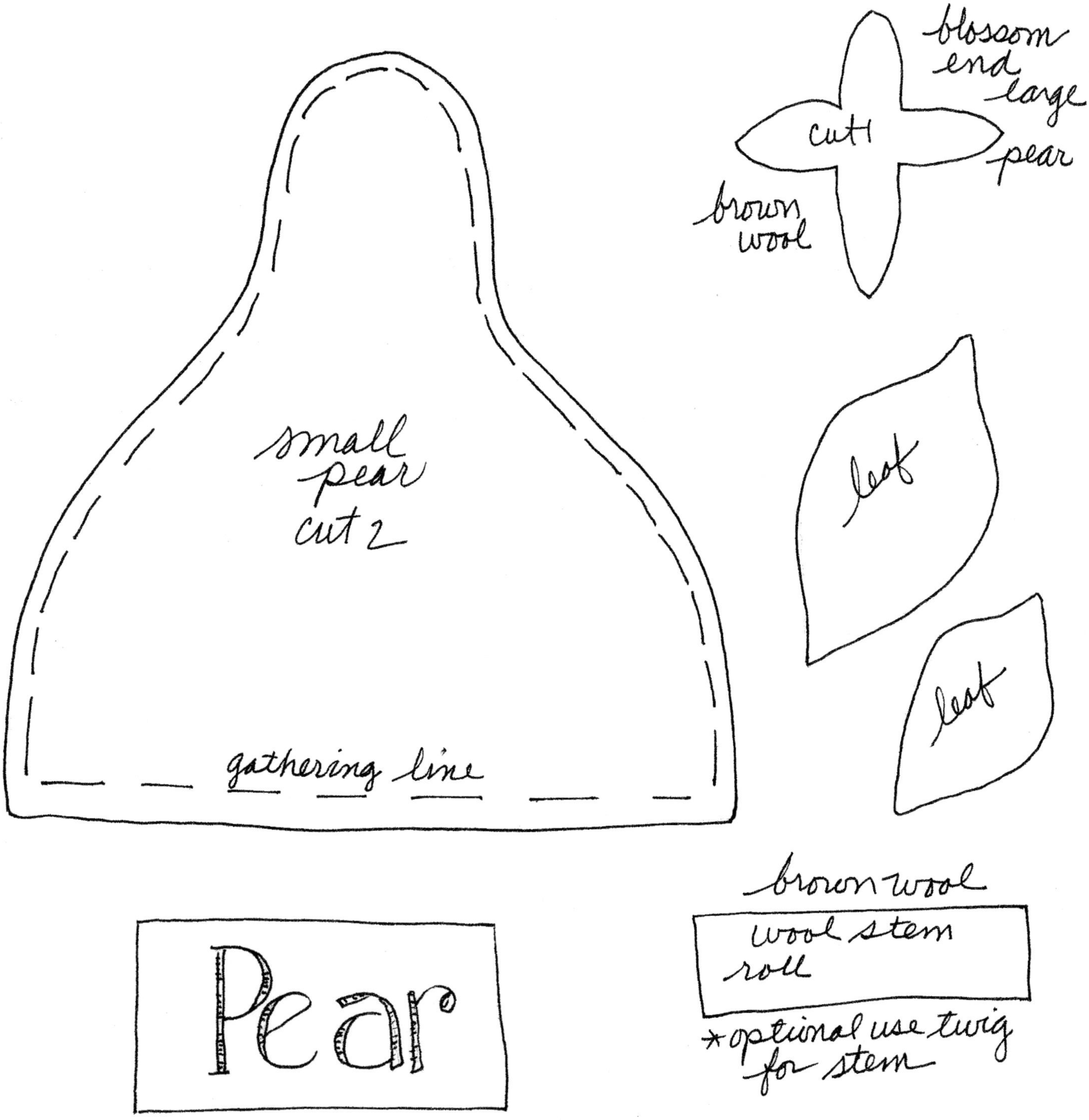

small
pear
cut 2

gathering line

Pear

blossom
end
large
pear

cut 1

brown
wool

leaf

leaf

brown wool

wool stem
roll

* optional use twig
for stem

Gourd Make-do Pincushion

9" x 6" (will vary with size of gourd)

This pincushion came about when I had the top portion of a dried gourd. I think I used the bottom part as a jack-o-lantern, but that was a long while ago. The shape of the gourd top reminded me of a pear and it would just need the bottom portion to be complete....

Materials needed

Dried gourd top
12" circle of black calico cotton fabric
Scraps of wool and velvet for leaf and blossom end
1 old button for the blossom end
20" ribbon
Scrap of cotton to "repair" stem
Cotton stuffing
Tacky glue

Assembly

Press under about 1/2" of the edge of the black calico cotton fabric circle: begin to gather stitch the folded edge all around the circle. Fill the inside of the gourd top with cotton stuffing, as well as a large handful in the center of the cotton circle. When you draw up the circle insert the cut edge of the gourd, continue to stuff it so the bottom is firmly filled out. Glue along the cut edge of the gourd where the gathered edge of your fabric will be attached, tighten the threads and secure a knot. Cut a leaf shape using the large pear leaf on page 84 as well as the blossom end from velvet or wool. Sew the stitches along the center of the leaf like a vein and draw the thread to scrunch

it up a bit. Glue the tip of the leaf at the base of the gourd stem. Stitch a button onto the blossom end and tack it into place at the bottom of the make-do. Tie a bow at the base of the stem with the ribbon. Put some glue on the stem and wrap it with a scrap strip of cotton to make a "repair". Use this as a pincushion or group it with the other pears.....

Punkins

12" x 12" Wool Appliqué Twig Stool Pad

I love pumpkins - they come in all colors and sizes. It wouldn't be autumn without them. I like to have a big old wooden bowl full of the small sugar pie pumpkins, as well as a great big Cinderella or the soft bluegreen ones. I then find it hard to get rid of them once winter (or even spring) has set in but from experience you do not want to let one get soft and rotten! Those unfortunate ones can take a finish off anything or stain a rug. Now that really sounds awful but they are so pretty and I do check them. One day they are just fine and the next day they just give up and you have a mess on your hands...

Enough of that, let me tell you why I used a twig stool. I have collected them for ages, finding them in antique shops or shows. Each stool is different, some more rustic than the next. All handmade, sometimes no two sides are the same on one stool: they are folky and funny. I have

even found some covered in interesting old linoleum or padded with fabric and straw as the stuffing. The one I picked for this project was square with the corners cut off. You could easily adapt this project to fit a rectangular stool or just make a pillow to toss on an old hickory chair.

Materials needed

12" x 12" textured brown/black wool for background and a 1" x 16" scrap for ties

12" x 12" pumpkin wool for pad backing

3-4 assorted wools: Army green, rusty brown, pumpkin, or dirty gold totaling 12" x 3" for letters/numbers

2" x 3" green wool for stem

5" x 8" rusty/pumpkin wool for pumpkin

3" x 7" rusty brown wool for pumpkin

3" x 7" plaid pumpkin wool for pumpkin

4" x 8" dirty gold wool for pumpkin

12" x 36" thin quilt batting

Tan sewing thread or thread of choice.

Hand sewing supplies

Assembly

I placed my stool upside down on top of a piece of newsprint and traced around the top to get the pad pattern size. Cut out background and backing wool along with pattern pieces - use the photo as a guide.

Cut out all the pieces on pages 90-91 and appliqué them in place on the background. Lay the backing out wrong side up, lay the batting on top. I found cutting the batting about 1/4" smaller all around works best. Now lay the appliquéd piece right side up and stitch all around, no need for fancy finishing as this is a rustic piece. I cut some strips 1/4" x 16" and tacked then to the edge of the pad where they may best tie to the stool. The legs or side supports work best for this.

PUNKIS

cut 2
→

Cut letters
from assorted colors:
gold, rust, brown,
pumpkin,
green

same
for →

$100

Top

#4
punkin
dirty
gold

slip edge under #3

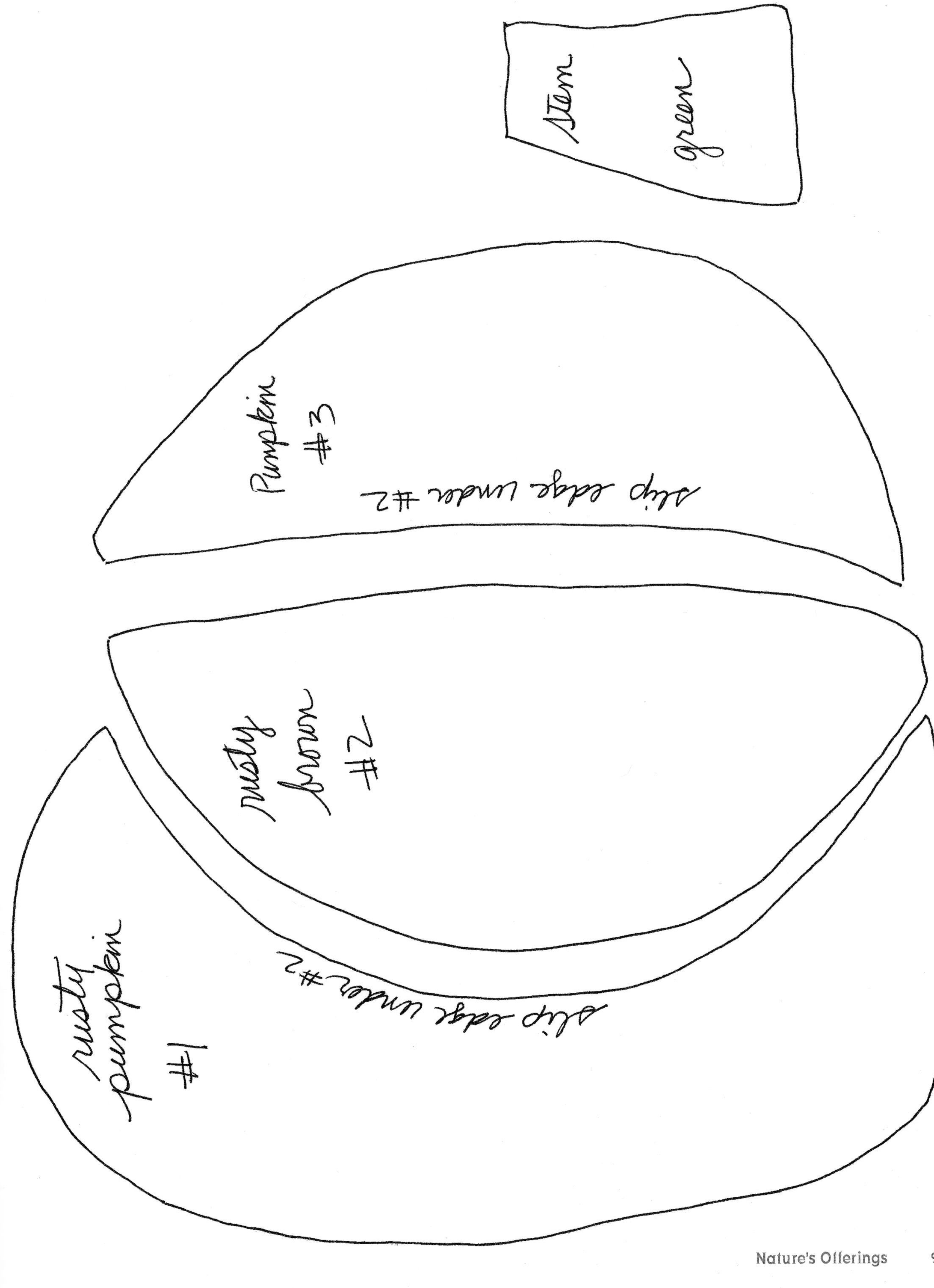

Stem
green

Pumpkin #3

Slip edge under #2

rusty green #2

rusty pumpkin #1

Slip edge under #2

Boughs of Holly

One of the wonderful evergreens we use during the holidays is holly. The shiny leaves and red berries are perfect for Christmas but look beautiful through the winter season. Just add a crock full of pine or spruce branches and you are set with a simple and easy decoration.

Both projects are similar, a branch with leaves, berries and tendrils.

The edges on the wool runner are left unfinished. I use several green wools for the leaves to add interest as well as two red wools for berries as well as brown wool for the branch. This project could easily be doubled in length by repeating the design with the large ends of the branches in the center, just increase your materials.

The embroidered piece I refer to as a "lay about", just a little piece of embroidery to accent a small place, by a candle stick, by that crock of greens, anywhere you might want an accent. This design could edge a table runner, pillow case, top edge of a Christmas stocking.

Linen embroidered pieces
13" x 4 1/2" and 8 1/2" x 4 1/2"

Materials needed
1/4 yard linen fabric
Embroidery floss - 1 skein each:
DMC 3777 red berries
    829 tan branch
    831 and 832 goldy-green colors for leaves
Hand sewing supplies, embroidery needle of your choice
Air erasable marking pen for pattern transfer

Assembly
All stitches are a satin stitch. First do the branch then leaves and berries. For the leaves, bring the needle and thread up thru the linen along the leaf edge and down through the vein line. Complete the stitching on one side of the leaf, then repeat for the other side. I have left these pieces unfinished on the edges but you may turn a small finished edge if you wish.

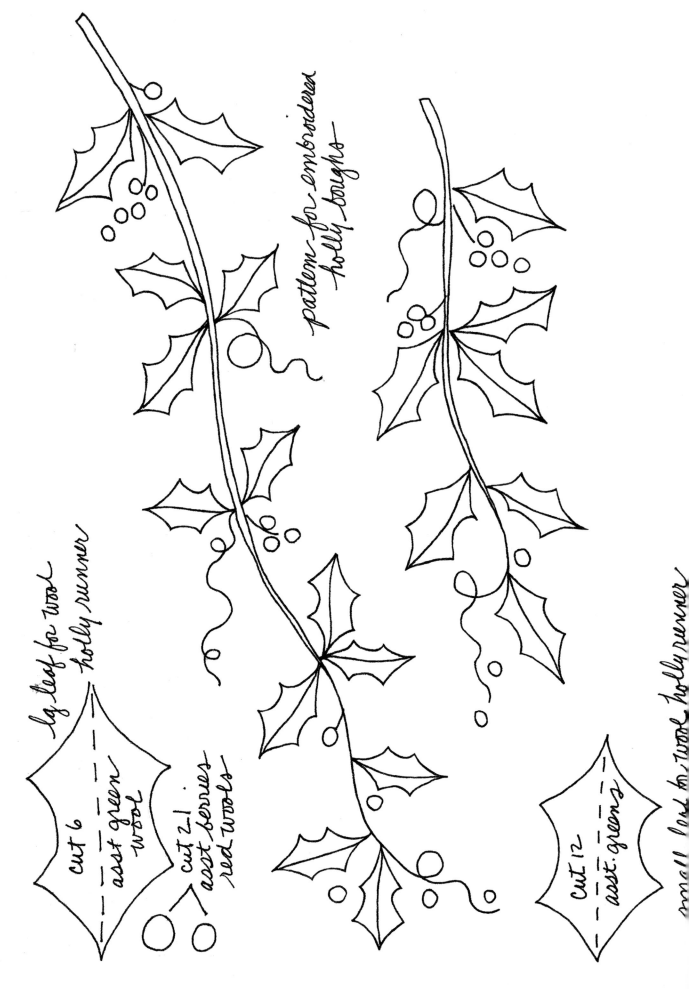

pattern for embroidered holly boughs

lg leaf for wool holly runner

cut 6
aost green wool

cut 21
aost berries red wool

cut 12
aast. greens

small leaf for mixture holly runner

Wool runner
9" x 29"

Materials needed

9" x 29" black wool for background

Approximately 9" x 12" total assorted green wools for leaves

12" x 3" brown wool for branch

1" x 3" scraps red wool for berries

Note: I used tan thread but you may want to match your thread colors

Hand sewing supplies

Assembly

Using the photo as your guide, join enough 3/8" strips of brown wool to make a 32" strip, tapering one end to a point. Cut a strip 8" x 1/4" and another 5" x 1/4" for the tendrils. Cut your leaves from the greens: 5 large and 12 small. Cut 21 assorted berries from the berry patterns on page 94. Pin and baste if desired and stitch in place. I just used a simple whip stitch.

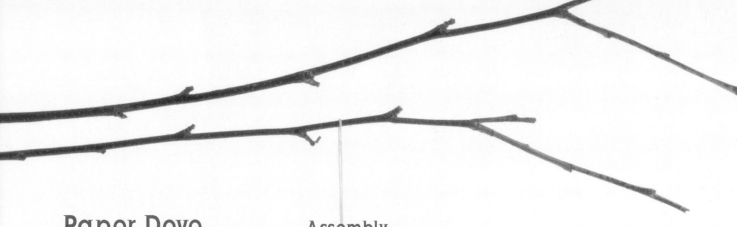

Paper Dove

This dove was made for Christmas one year using photocopies of an old deed. You can find interesting papers at scrapbooking stores.

Materials needed

4" x 6" manila folder or card stock bird body

8 1/2" x 11" journal or printed paper of choice for bird

Glue stick

Scissors

Pencil

Needle and white thread

Assembly

Cut out one bird body from manila folder or card stock. Cut out 2 bird bodies from printed paper. Be sure to flip over the pattern so you will have paper to fit both sides of the bird. Use the glue stick to glue the printed paper to both sides of the bird body. Cut out the tail feathers, fold in half as shown. Clip the end of the tail into sections and curl these with a pencil, then glue to the tail mark on the pattern, Cut out the wings: fold as shown to fit over top edge of the bird, then fold up on dashed line. Glue the wings to the bird, using the mark on the pattern as a guide. To hang the dove: you want it to hang balanced, so insert the needle where you think is the center. See if the bird balances on your needle. If not, make adjustments as necessary. Once the center is found, string a length of thread through the dove: knot and hang.

This dove could be used at Valentine's Day, too. Cut a small heart out of paper, thread a length of thread through the heart and the beak of the dove. You may have to adjust the balance, if so just move the hanging thread.

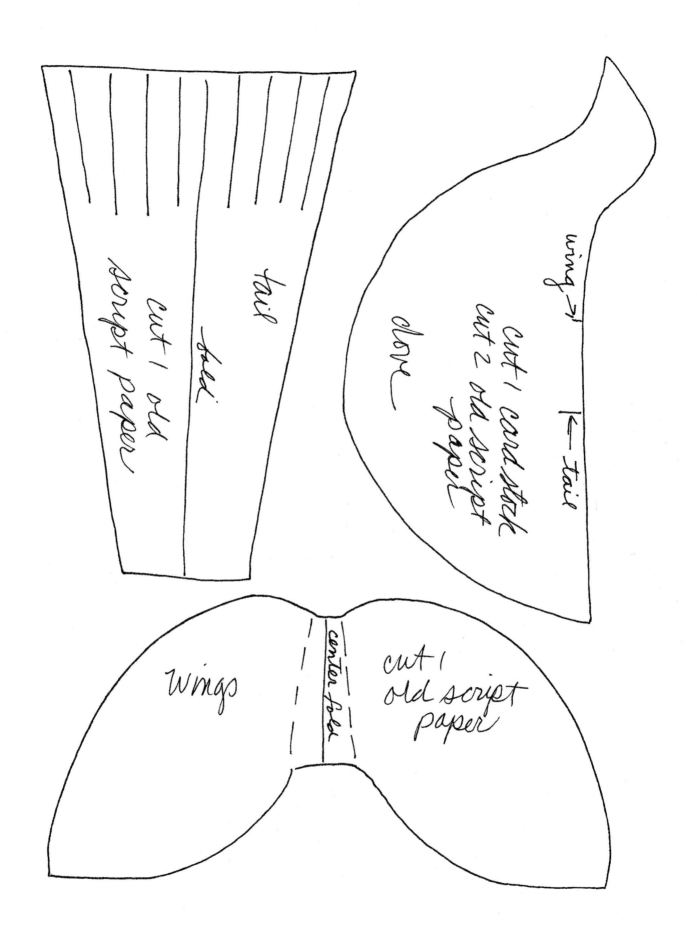

tail

fold

cut 1 old
script paper

wing →

← tail

cut 1 card stock
cut 2 old script
paper

dove

wings

center fold

cut 1
old script
paper

Templates

Flower Basket Hooked Rug pattern

1835
Primitive Flower Basket
Maggie Bonanomi

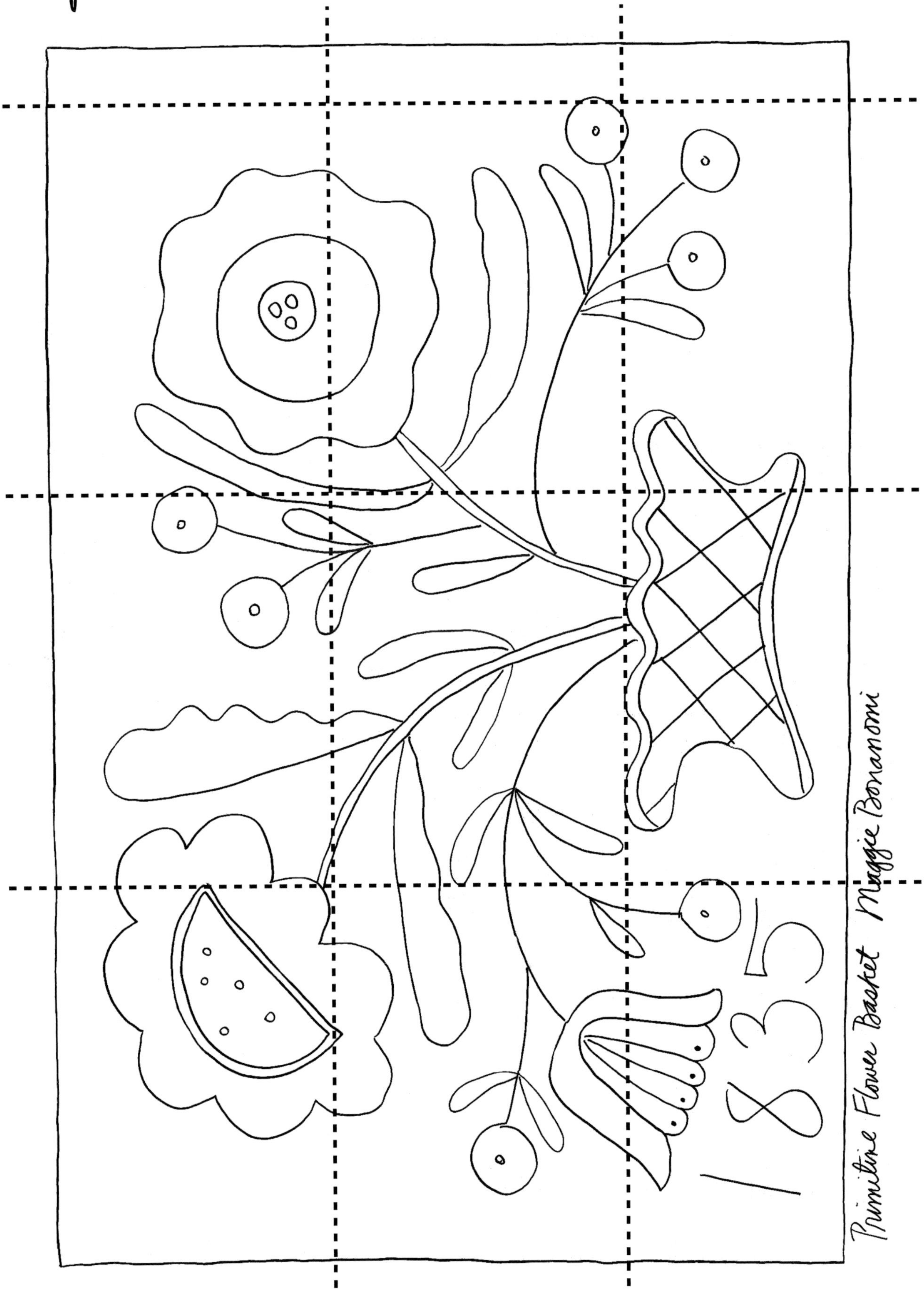

Flower Basket Hooked
Rug pattern

Top Left

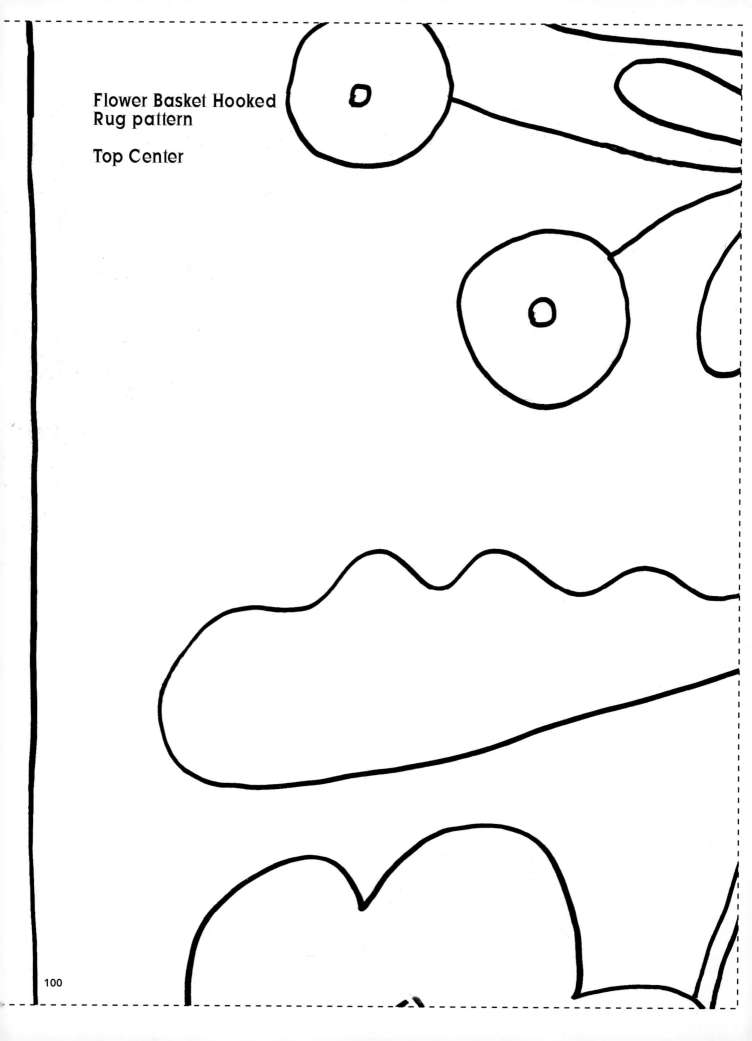

Flower Basket Hooked
Rug pattern

Top Center

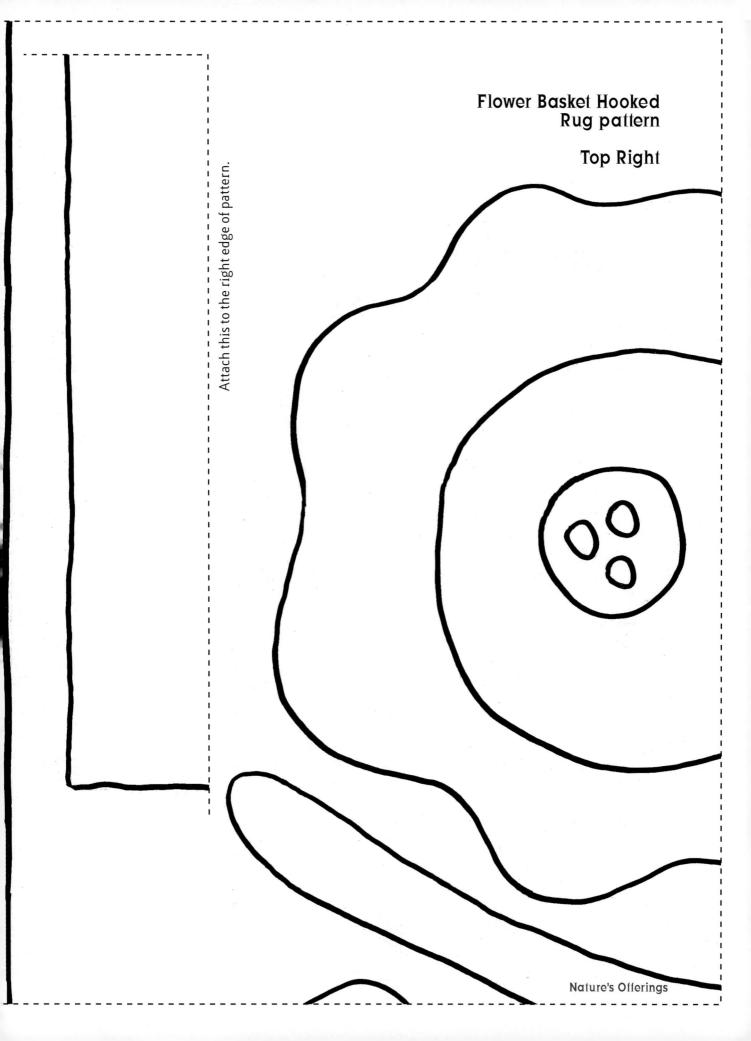

Flower Basket Hooked
Rug pattern

Top Right

Attach this to the right edge of pattern.

Nature's Offerings

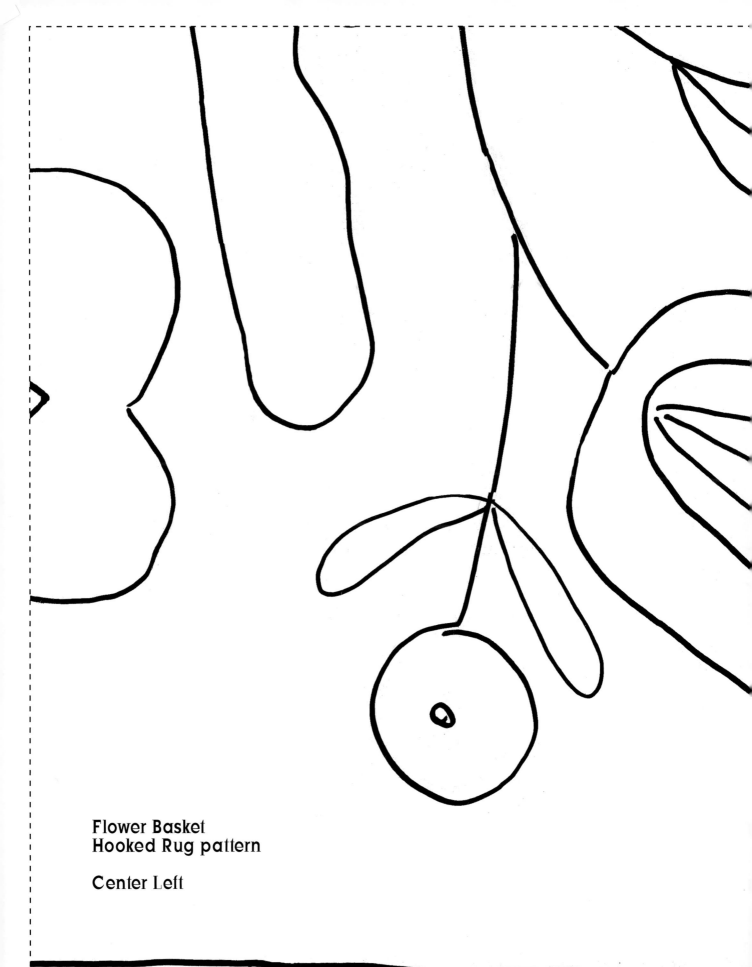

**Flower Basket
Hooked Rug pattern**

Center Left

Flower Basket
Hooked Rug
pattern

Center

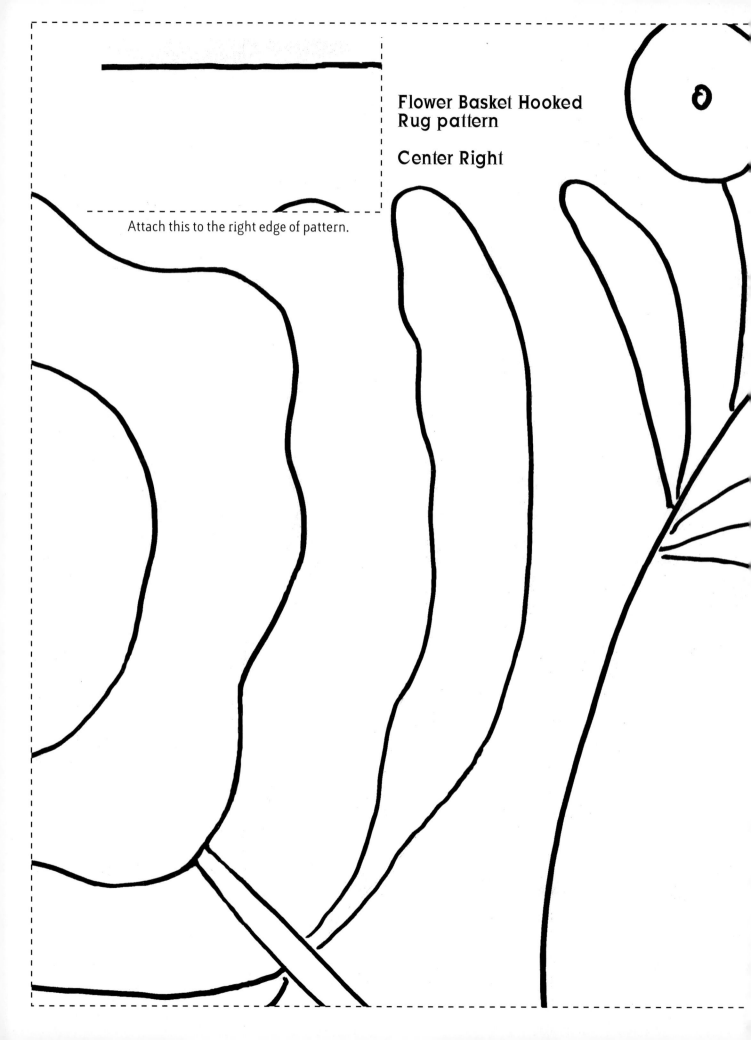

Flower Basket Hooked Rug pattern

Center Right

Attach this to the right edge of pattern.

**Flower Basket
Hooked Rug pattern**

Bottom Left

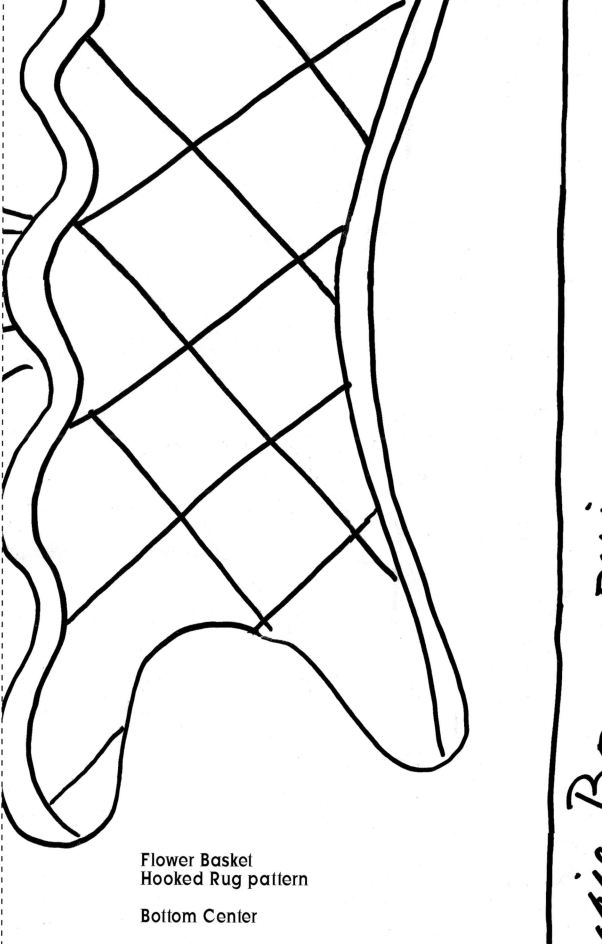

Flower Basket
Hooked Rug pattern

Bottom Center

Maggie Bonanomi

Flower Basket Hooked Rug pattern

Bottom Right

Attach this to the right edge of pattern.

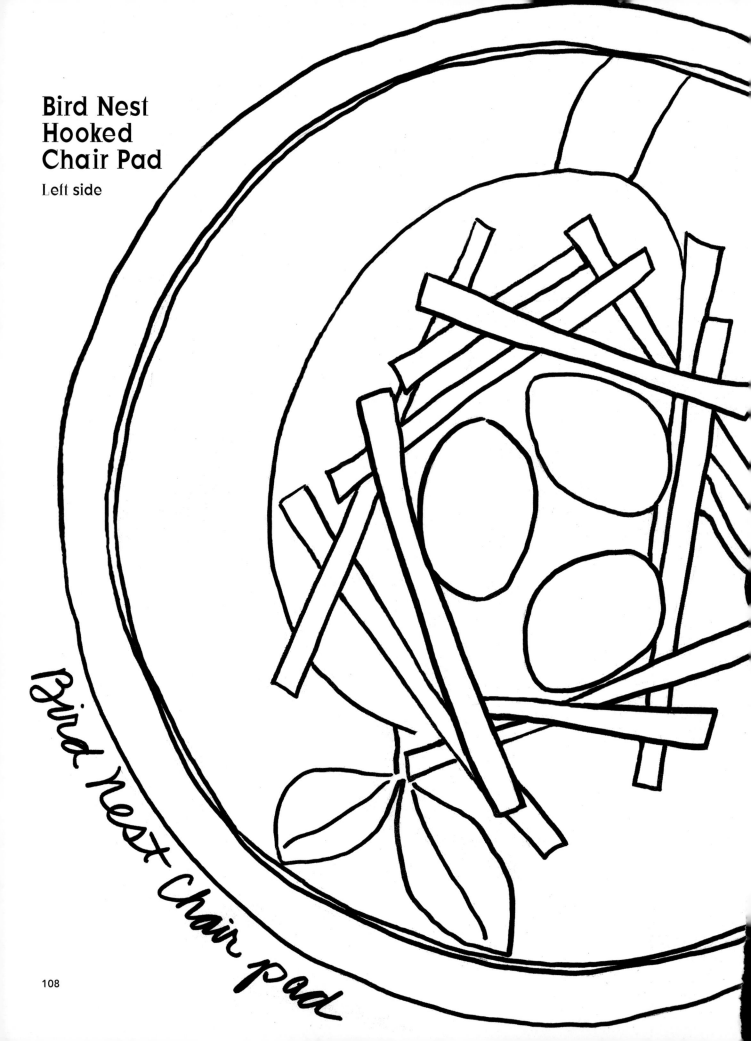

Bird Nest Hooked Chair Pad

Left side

Bird nest chair pad

Bird Nest Hooked Chair Pad

Right side

Bird Nest Chair pad

For lo, the winter is past;
the rain is over and gone;
The flowers appear on earth;
the time of the singing of
birds is come.

Song of Solomon 2:10-12

ABCDE
FGHIJK
LMNOP
QRSTU

V W X Y
Z 1 2
3 4 5 6
7 8 9 0

Resources

Resources Listed in projects:

Winter's Garden Bed Cover, page 16
Hobb's cotton batting
Craft Products Division
PO Box 2521
Waco, Texas 76702-2521
www.hobbsbondedfibers.com
254-741-0040

DMC thread
Available at quilt and
craft stores

Silly Rabbit, page 38 and Autumn Pears, page 80
Parakeet gravel and grit can be found in pet stores. This is easier to work with than a 50-pound bag of sand.

Large Green Pear, page 80 and Pear Ornament, page 83
Gauzy muslin (undyed)
Maggie Bonanomi
1006 Highland Ave
Lexington, MO 64067
660-232-4406
maggiebonanomi@juno.com

Quilt Shops: fabric, wool, and cross stitch supplies

Country Sampler
133 East Jefferson St.
Spring Green, WI 53588
608-588-2510
sgcountrysampler.com

Quilters Station
806 SW Blue Parkway
Lee's Summit, MO 64063
816-525-8955
quiltersstation.com

The Buggy Barn
28848 Tramm Rd. N
Reardan, WA 99029
509-796-2188
buggybarnquilts.com

Rug hooking supplies

Emma Lou Lais
Emma Lou's Primitives
5015 Chouteau Street
Shawnee, KS 66226
913-745-5605
emmalousprimitives.com

Rhonda Manley
16221 NE 116 St.
Liberty, Missouri 64068
816-781-6844
rhonda@blacksheepwoolde-signs.com
www.blacksheepwooldesigns.com

Blackberry Primitives
www.blackberryprimitives.com
Wool@Blackberryprimitives.com
Cindi 402-423-8464
Tonja 402-792-2014

Anita White
12835 Perry
Overland Park, KS 66213
913-685-0180
anitahooksrugs@yahoo.com

Rustic Rugs
Judy Cripps
3212 SW Arrowhead Rd.
Topeka, KS 66614
785-273-2093
www.judycripps.com
rusticrugs@judycripps.com

Saltbox Primitive Woolens
Patty Wallace
30173 Shawnee Bend (mailing address)
303 Seminary (shop location)
Warsaw, MO. 65355
660-438-6002
saltboxwoolens@embarqmail.com
www.mountainhandcrafts.com

Black Horse Antiques
Janice Lee
29049 Garvin Road
Valley, NE 68064
402-359-2699
www.janicelee.biz
info@janicelee.biz

Baskets of Wool
Cammie Bruce
Lincoln, NE
402-742-3071
basketsofwool@alltel.net
www.basketsofwool.com

Woolgatherings
Rachel Cochran
910 Main St
Lexington, MO 64067
660-259-2320
woolgathering@embarqmail.com

Simply Butternut
Maggie Bonanomi
Lexington, MO 64067
660-232-4406
maggiebonanomi@juno.com

Antique Shops: old blankets, fabrics and antiques

Bruce Burstert LLC
1010 Main St., lower level
Lexington, MO 64067
Carl Wheat: 816-267-2222
Bruce Burstert: 816-665-7989

Missouri River Antique Co.
912 Main St.
Lexington, MO 64067
660-259-3097

Greenwood Mercantile
409 Main
Greenwood, MO 64034
816-537-7033

Country Heritage & Friends
16005 Allendale Lake Rd.
Greenwood, MO 64034
816-537-8863
816-537-7822

Friends Together Antiques
4038 E. Broadway
Columbia, MO 65201
573-442-6759

White Horse Antiques, rug hooking
505 Third St.
Rocheport, MO 65279
573-698-2088

Local Interest Sites

Battle of Lexington State
Historic Site
PO Box 6
Lexington, MO 64067
Janae Fuller
Resource Manager

Lexington Tourism Bureau
www.visitlexingtonmo.com